MW00887401

THE GERMAN CHRISTMAS BAKE BOOK

The German Kitchen

Published by Mindful Publishing

Mindful Publishing on Instagram: @mindful_publishing

The German Kitchen on Instagram: @german.recipes

TABLE OF CONTENT

Baked apple cake

raisins - yeast plait

Butter cookies

Snowballs

Cinnamon Cookie Balls

Ginger - hazelnut - cubes

Spice Cuts

Chocolate cookies

Tea Bread

Stollen confectionery

Snickerdoodles

Christmas cake

Oranges - Chocolates - Cookies

Hazelnut - Cookies

Hazelnut - croissant

chocolate - mint - cookies

Chocolate Bread

Butter buttons

Gingerbread Hearts

Apple Speculoos Muffins

Baiser

Rum Balls

Lebkuchen

Cinnamon stars

Cinnamon buns - Biscuits

Macadamia - Biscuits

Aladushki

Stuffed poppy seed cookies

Nougat - Cookies

shortbread cookies

Cinnamon balls

Mascarpone cream with cinnamon stars

Chocolate - Walnut - Buttons

chocolate - marzipan cake

Christmas cookies

Chocolate Oranges - Kipferl

Angel's eyes

Chocolate snowballs

shortbread cookies

Christstollen - Gugelhupf

Cinnamon wafers

Butter cookies

Oatmeal cookies

Springerle

Lebkuchen - Muffins

Ginger cookies with chocolate icing

White mulled wine

Peanut cookies

Egg liqueur - nut coins

Peanut - Cookies

Mulled wine spice cake with chocolate

Cinnamon Brownies

Nougat rods

Cashew-Toffees

Eggnog - Stars

Red wine cake

Shaking-Lebkuchen

Nut wreath with short pastry

Nutella cookies

Walnut coins

Marzipan custard

Nougat - Curd Stollen

Round pepper nuts

Lebkuchen Brownies

Fig Spirals

White Mousse au chocolat

Peanut - Caramel - Macarons

Stuffed orange cookies

Ice confectionery

Aniseed cookies

Spaghetti Biscuits

Vanilla - Bits

Nut bags

Baked apple casserole with marzipan

Rum Balls

Mousse au chocolat with orange scent

Coconut cookies

Welfenspeise

Sour cream - Kringel with sugar

Pumpkin seed croissant

Spice Balls

shortbread cookies

Christmas-Cookies

Lebkuchen parfait with red wine pear

Nuss-Nougat-Stangen

White rum balls

yeast men

Anise buttons with chocolate

Chocolates - Crème brûlée with spicy oranges

Red wine cookies

Balsamic - Nut - Pieces

Christmas chocolate

Mulled wine cake with cinnamon cream topping

Cocoa cookies with christmas spices

Christmas Dessert

Cornflakes - Biscuits

Vanilla pear with chocolate-maronic cream

Quark balls

Almond cake

Baked apples in walnut coat

Cinnamon ice cream with pears and gingerbread sauce

GINGERBREAD

Working time approx. 45 Minutes
Total time approx. 45 Minutes

ingredients
6 eggs
180 g sugar, brown
2 tablespoons honey
2 teaspoons cinnamon
1 teaspoon gingerbread spice
1 pinch of salt
250 g ground almond
250 g hazelnuts, ground
200 g candied orange peel, crushed a little more in a mixer
200 g candied lemon peel, still a little bit crushed in the mixer
wafers, 70 or 90 mm
200 g chocolate coating

preparation
Beat eggs, sugar and honey until frothy. Mix in the rest of the dough ingredients. Spread the dough flat on the wafers (makes approx. 30 pcs/90 mm or approx. 40 pcs/70 mm).

Put it on the baking tray lined with baking paper. Bake with top and bottom heat at 150°, approx. 20 minutes.

After cooling down, cover with chocolate coating if necessary.

STOLLEN CONFECTIONERY

vegetarian

Working time approx. 30 Minutes
Cooking/baking time approx. 15 Minutes
Total time approx. 45 Minutes

ingredients
200 g butter
150 g sugar
300 g quark
600 g flour
2 teaspoons cinnamon
1 package baking powder
100 g almond, chopped
100 g raisins
100 g candied orange peel
100 g candied lemon peel
rum at your discretion
1 orange peel
250 g powdered sugar
200 g butter

preparation
Results in about 80 pieces
Mix the flour with baking powder and spices, put aside. Cream the butter with the sugar, stir in the quark and orange peel. Add the flour mixture, stir in briefly, then add almonds, raisins, candied orange peel, candied lemon peel and enough rum to make a

smooth, malleable but not sticky dough.

Now heat the oven to 180°C circulating air. Take off about walnut-sized portions of vpm dough, flatten them a bit on the palm
of your hand and form them into small stollen. Place on the prepared trays and bake for 10 - 15 minutes until the surface turns
golden yellow.

In the meantime, sieve the powdered sugar onto a plate or plat-
ter and melt the butter in a small saucepan. Turn the mini stollen while still warm in the butter and then roll in the powdered
sugar. Leave to stand for at least one day in a tightly closed tin.

It is also possible to form slightly larger mini stollen (see pic-
ture), then the baking time is 20 - 25 minutes.

SPICE CAKE

vegetarian

Total time approx. 30 Minutes

ingredients
4 egg
300 g sugar
½ Package gingerbread spice
1/2 teaspoon nutmeg
1 teaspoon cinnamon
2 tablespoons cocoa powder
1 bottle of rum aroma
350 g flour
1 package baking powder
¼ Liters of oil
¼ Liters of mineral water
100 g chocolate, grated (you can also use grated chocolate)
2 pack powdered sugar
Carnation

preparation
Prepare a sponge mixture from the above ingredients (except powdered sugar), spread on a baking tray and bake at 200 °C for about 25 minutes,
Let the cake cool down and make a cake dough from the powdered sugar and spread it on the cake.
If you leave out the spices and put a chocolate icing on it after baking, it is a delicious cake for children.

GINGERBREAD TIRAMISU

vegetarian

Working time approx. 30 Minutes
Rest period approx. 6 hours
Cooking/baking time approx. 10 Minutes
Total time approx. 6 hours 40 Minutes

ingredients
200 g gingerbread, pretzels, stars, hearts
1 jar of sour cherries, capacity 680 g drained weight
250 g Mascarpone
250 g quark
200 g sour cream
100 g sugar
50 ml Amaretto
1 package of custard powder

For sprinkling:
Cocoa powder

preparation
Crush the gingerbread (I use the blender to do this) and fill it into an oven dish. Pour the sour cherries into a sieve and let them drain. Boil the collected cherry juice with a tablespoon of sugar and the pudding powder to a pudding and mix it with the drained cherries, let it cool down and then spread it on the gingerbread.

Mix mascarpone, quark, sour cream, alcohol and the remaining sugar. Then pour everything onto the cherry mixture, smooth it down and put it in a cool place to soak.

Sprinkle with cocoa before serving.

CHOCOLATE - ALMOND - SLICES

vegetarian

Total time approx. 30 Minutes

ingredients
6 medium sized egg
250 g butter
250 g sugar
100 g flour
250 g almond, finely ground
250 g chocolate coating, semi-bitter, finely grated
1/2 teaspoon cinnamon powder
1 package cake glaze (chocolate glaze)
60 Almond, for decoration

preparation
Results in approx. 60 pieces
Cream eggs, sugar and butter. Add flour, almonds, chocolate coating, cinnamon and a pinch of salt and stir well. Smooth the mixture on a baking tray lined with baking paper.

Bake in the oven at 180° on the middle shelf for about 25 minutes until the surface is dry and no longer shiny.

While still warm, cut into approx. 4 x 4 cm pieces, let them cool on the baking tray and cover with the chocolate icing. Decorate with the whole almonds.

OAT COOKIES

vegetarian

Total time approx. 20 Minutes

ingredients
120 g butter
120 g sugar
1 egg
1 pinch of salt
90 g oat flakes
80 g ground almond
80 g flour
1 teaspoon baking powder
1 pinch of cinnamon

preparation
Cream soft butter with sugar and egg (whisk), mix remaining ingredients separately, then gradually add to butter mixture. Don't worry, the result is more of a paste than a smooth dough!

Preheat the oven to 180 degrees and place baking paper on the baking tray.

Use a spoon to cut off some of the dough, form small balls by hand and place them on the prepared baking tray with a wide gap between them. (approx. 10 - 14 pcs. per baking tray). Bake on the middle shelf for approx. 12 - 15 minutes. Take out at the latest when the edges are visibly browned.

Carefully remove the still soft cookies from the tray and let them cool down.

CHRISTMAS CAKE

vegetarian

Total time approx. 35 Minutes

ingredients
130 g butter
90 g sugar
1 egg yolk
½ Lemon, grated zest
150 g flour
1 package pudding powder, vanilla
7 drops of bitter almond aroma
50 g ground almond
100 g fruits, dried, finely chopped (figs, dates, candied lemon peel, candied orange peel)

preparation
Knead butter, sugar, egg, lemon, flour, pudding powder, aroma, almonds into a shortcrust pastry, finally knead in the fruits, form walnut-sized pieces into balls and place on a baking tray covered with baking paper, bake in a preheated oven at 160° hot air for approx. 8-10 min.

GINGERBREAD FROM MILK ROLL

vegetarian

Total time approx. 1 hour

ingredients
8 rolls, (milk roll)
350 ml water
350 g sugar
3 large egg
1 package gingerbread spice
1 package baking powder
100 g apricot, dried
100 g prune
300 g ground almonds or hazelnuts
100 g almond, chopped
40 wafers, large
Powdered sugar
Rum

preparation
Makes about 40 gingerbreads.
Break up the milk rolls and soak them in the water.

Whip the sugar and eggs until creamy and gradually stir in the gingerbread spice, baking powder, nuts, almonds and baking powder. Cut the dried fruit into very small pieces (I use a food processor for this), also stir in and work in the soaked rolls with the dough hook (do not squeeze out before!).

Put the dough with a tablespoon on the baking wafers and bake at 180°C circulating air for about 20 minutes.

While still hot, spread a thick icing sugar-rum glaze on the dough, then let it cool down.

APPLE PIE

vegetarian

Total time approx. 2 hours

430 calories

ingredients
80 g butter or margarine
205 g sugar
2 packs vanilla sugar
3 egg
100 g flour
1 teaspoon baking powder
3 tablespoons of milk
50 g powdered sugar
500 g apples
2 tablespoons lemon juice
175 ml apple juice
1 pack dessert sauce vanilla flavor for cooking
6 sheets gelatine, white
300 g yoghurt
250 g Mascarpone
250 g whipped cream
1 tablespoon cinnamon, to decorate

preparation
Beat the fat until foamy. Stir in 80 g sugar and 1 packet of vanilla sugar.
Separate 2 eggs. Add egg yolks and 1 egg to the fat-sugar mixture and whip until creamy. Mix flour and baking powder and stir in.

Add milk. Grease a springform pan (26 cm diameter). Smooth the dough in it.

Beat egg white until stiff, add powdered sugar. Spread the beaten egg white on the dough in the form. Bake in the pre-heated oven (175° C) for about 30 minutes. Take out and let cool down.

Peel and quarter apples and remove the core. Cut apples into small cubes and boil them up with lemon juice, apple juice and 50 g sugar. Cook for 3 - 4 minutes. Stir the sauce powder in a little cold water until smooth and thicken the apples. Let the apple compote cool down.

Soak the gelatine for about 10 minutes. Mix yoghurt, mascarpone, 1 P vanilla sugar and 75 g sugar.

Squeeze the gelatine, dissolve at low heat. Stir into the yoghurt-mascarpone mixture. Fold in apple compote.

Remove the cake base from the mould and enclose it with a cake ring. Spread the apple-mascarpone cream on the cake base and smooth it down. Whip the cream until stiff and spread on the cake. Chill the cake for 4 - 5 hours.

Loosen the cake ring. Cut out a tail star from a paper. Place the paper on the cake and sprinkle the star with cinnamon. Remove the paper carefully.

NUT CORNERS

vegetarian

Working time approx. 45 Minutes
Cooking/baking time approx. 25 Minutes
Total time approx. 1 hour 10 Minutes

ingredients
For the dough:
130 g butter or margarine
130 g sugar
2 egg
300 g flour
1 teaspoon baking powder

For the flooring:
4 tablespoons apricot jam
200 g butter or margarine
200 g sugar
2 packs vanilla sugar
200 g hazelnuts, ground
200 g hazelnuts, chopped
4 tablespoons of water
cake glaze, chocolate

preparation
The quantity is sufficient for about 32 pieces.

Prepare knead dough and roll out on a greased baking tray.
Spread apricot jam on the rolled out dough.

Heat butter, sugar and vanilla sugar until the sugar is dissolved.

Stir nuts together with water into the butter-sugar mixture. Pour onto the dough.

Bake in the preheated oven at 175° C top/bottom heat for approx. 25 minutes. While still warm, first cut into rectangles, then into triangles and dip the corners in couverture or chocolate icing.

RUM - MOONS

vegetarian

Total time approx. 30 Minutes

6836 calories

ingredients
250 g butter or margarine, soft
180 g sugar
6 medium sized egg
140 g walnuts, grated
140 g chocolate (dark chocolate), melted
160 g flour
For the glaze:
250 g powdered sugar
8 tablespoons rum
Grease for the sheet metal
Flour for the sheet

preparation
Results in about 120 pieces.
Preheat the oven to 190°C. Separate the eggs. Beat the egg whites until very stiff. Cream the egg yolks with butter and sugar. Stir in nuts and melted chocolate. Stir in the flour and half of the egg whites. Finally fold in the remaining snow.

Grease and flour a baking tray or better use baking paper. Spread the mixture evenly. Bake on the middle rack at 190°C for about 25 - 30 minutes (test with sticks!). Turn the cake over, remove the baking parchment.

For the icing, stir the powdered sugar with rum until smooth and spread it on the hot cake. Let it dry for a few minutes.

Use a round cookie cutter (4.5 cm diameter) to cut a semicircular piece from the long side. Now move the cookie cutter further and further forward to cut out moons. This way you have very little waste. Let the finished moons cool down and enjoy.

STOLLEN CONFECTIONERY

vegetarian

Working time approx. 30 Minutes
Rest period approx. 2 hours
Cooking/baking time approx. 10 Minutes
Total time approx. 2 hours 40 Minutes

6908 calories

ingredients
For the dough:
100 g raisins
100 g apricot, dried, finely diced
50 g candied lemon peel
100 g almond, chopped
100 g marzipan
150 g sugar
1 bag of baking powder
2 sachets vanilla sugar
2 tablespoons rum, or 2 x rum aroma
300 g butter, or margarine
2 medium sized egg
600 g flour

To decorate:
2 sachets vanilla sugar
3 tablespoons powdered sugar
½ teaspoon cinnamon powder

preparation

Knead all ingredients for the dough with your hands to a smooth dough. Form long rolls from the dough, wrap in cling film and put in the fridge for 2 hours.

Divide the rolls into 2-3 cm pieces. Place them on a baking tray and bake in the oven preheated to 180 C° for about 8-10 minutes. When they are slightly brown, they are ready. Put them on a cake rack to cool down and sprinkle them with the sugar-cinnamon mixture while they are still hot.

WALNUT HEARTS

vegetarian

Working time approx. 1 hour 30 Minutes
Rest period approx. 1 hour
Cooking/baking time approx. 15 Minutes
Total time approx. 2 hours 45 Minutes

ingredients
200 g butter
125 g powdered sugar
1 package vanilla sugar
1 egg yolk
60 g walnuts, grated
300 g flour
400 g marzipan paste
Powdered sugar, to roll out
Apricot Jam
400 g chocolate coating
Walnuts, halves, for decoration

preparation
Mix the butter with the powdered sugar, vanilla sugar, egg yolks and the grated walnuts. Gradually knead in the flour, cover the dough and let it rest in the refrigerator for 1 hour.

Then roll out on a floured baking board, cut out hearts or round shapes, place on a baking tray covered with baking paper and bake in a preheated oven at 150 °C for about 15 - 20 minutes until light yellow.

Knead the marzipan paste with powdered sugar, roll out thinly and cut out as well. Spread the cooled cookies with apricot jam, cover with marzipan cookies, cover with chocolate coating and decorate with 1/2 walnut.

MARZIPAN - CURD - STOLLEN

vegetarian

Total time approx. 40 Minutes

ingredients

375 g raisins
100 ml rum or apple juice
375 g wheat flour
4 teaspoons baking powder
125 g sugar
1 package of vanilla sugar or vanilla sugar, homemade
1 small bottle of butter-vanilla flavor and possibly rum flavor
1/2 teaspoon cardamom, ground
1/2 teaspoon mace, ground
1 teaspoon orange peel, grated
250 g low-fat curd cheese
1 egg
1 egg yolk
150 g butter, soft
100 g candied lemon peel
200 g ground almond
100 g marzipan paste
100 g butter, melted
Powdered sugar

preparation
Soak the raisins in rum or apple juice overnight.

THE GERMAN CHRISTMAS BAKE BOOK

Drain the raisins first before preparation.

Mix the flour with baking powder and sieve into a mixing bowl. Add sugar, vanillin sugar, butter-vanilla flavor (if you used apple juice, add rum flavor), cardamom, mace, orange peel, curd, egg, egg yolk and the softened butter and work everything through with the mixer on highest setting for about 5 minutes. Then place the dough on a lightly floured work surface and press a depression into it. Add candied lemon peel, ground almonds and rum raisins and work everything into a smooth dough. If it sticks too much (depending on how much liquid the raisins have drawn), add some flour.

Roll out the dough rectangularly to about 30 x 20 cm. Knead the marzipan well until oil comes out and roll out to a rectangle of 30 x 15 cm. Place the marzipan on the dough so that some of the dough remains free on the long sides. Do not roll the dough too loosely from the longer side, lay it on the seam and form it into a stollen. Place the stollen on triple (important, otherwise it will burn from below!) baking paper and bake at 150°C for 50-60 minutes. Check in between if it gets too dark. If so, cover with aluminium foil.

Take the stollen out and spread with half of the melted butter. Sprinkle with powdered sugar immediately. Repeat the process several times.

Wrap the cooled stollen tightly in parchment or baking paper and additionally wrap it in aluminum foil. This way it will last for several weeks. I usually bake the stollen two to three weeks before Christmas and leave it to rest in a cool place until then.

BUTTERSTOLLEN

vegetarian

Working time approx. 30 Minutes
Rest period approx. 1 Day 2 hours
Cooking/baking time approx. 1 hour
Total time approx. 1 Day 3 hours 30 Minutes

6813 calories

ingredients
500 g wheat flour, 550
100 g milk
42 g yeast, fresh, 1 cube
275 g butter, room temperature
75 g sugar, finest sugar
1 bag of vanilla sugar, bourbon
5 g salt
fresh lemon peel
300 g raisins
8 cl rum, brown 54, approx. 70g
75 g almond, chopped
50 g candied lemon peel
25 g candied orange peel
50 g butter (sweet cream), liquid, for spreading
2 tablespoons sugar, finest, to sprinkle
1 cup powdered sugar and 1 teaspoon cornflour, to dust

preparation
First, the raisins are washed, well drained and placed in a lock-able box together with the rum. This is left to stand for at least

24 hours. The rum should be completely absorbed, shaking it occasionally helps.

On the day of baking, put the flour into the mixing bowl and press a deep depression into it. Add the milk and mix the yeast milk with just enough flour to form a soft pre-dough. Cover the dough with the flour that is not needed for the pre-dough and let it rise for 30-90 minutes, depending on the temperature of the milk. The volume must increase significantly and the surface must be clearly cracked.

In the meantime, boil the chopped almonds in boiling water, leave to stand for 5 minutes and then drain well. They only come to the dough later.

When the pre-dough has risen, add butter at room temperature, sugar, vanilla sugar, salt and lemon peel and knead the stollen dough, which is then left to rise for 30 minutes. Now knead the fruits and the almonds and form the stollen. If necessary add some more flour if the dough is too moist due to the rum raisins.

In the meantime, the oven is preheated to 180 - 200 °C top/ bottom heat. The more stollen you put into the oven at once, the hotter you have to preheat. The stollen is placed on a cold baking tray lined with baking paper, wiped with cold water and placed in the oven without piece fermentation, which is immediately reduced to 170°C. The baking time is 60 minutes. The baking time is the most important factor here, the temperature may have to be adjusted. If it is too dark, it will dry out, if it is too light, it is possible that it is not cooked through and is therefore slippery inside.

Afterwards the stollen is coated with liquid butter and sugared. Do not move the stollen, it is still very fragile. The baking tray is best put back into the cooled down oven. The next day, dust the stollen with powdered sugar and starch mixture. The starch prevents the powdered sugar from turning yellow.

Now the finished stollen is packed nicely. The best way to do this is to put it into a special stollen tube. If necessary, you can also use cling film or aluminum foil plus freezer bag. The stollen should now pull through a little, but not necessarily 2 - 4 weeks as often described. 2 - 3 days are completely sufficient, it is best after one week.

If you don't like candied lemon peel/orange peel or if you like marzipan, I have 3 more delicious variations for you:

1. for a marzipan stollen instead of the almonds, candied lemon peel and candied orange peel, wrap 200 g of marzipan paste in strips in the stollen, or roll it up as a marzipan plate and reduce the sugar to 50 g.

2. for an almond stollen instead of the candied lemon peel and candied orange peel, double the amount, i.e. 150 g almonds, and work into the dough.

3. for a sweet almond bread, also leave out the raisins, but put 300 g of almonds in rum and butter the finished bread, do not sugar it and do not dust it with powdered sugar.
Translated with www.DeepL.com/Translator (free version)

RASPBERRY DESSERT WITH SPEKULATIUS

vegetarian

Working time approx. 20 Minutes
Rest period approx. 4 hours
Total time approx. 4 hours 20 Minutes

420 calories

ingredients
200 ml cream
250 g quark
250 g Mascarpone
125 g sugar
1 package vanilla sugar
350 g raspberries
250 g speculoos

preparation
Whip the cream. Mix quark, mascarpone, sugar and vanilla sugar. Fold in the cream.

In a sufficiently high square or round bowl cover the bottom with three or four tablespoons of cream. Spread a layer of Spekulatius on top, whole or broken into pieces. Spread half of the remaining cream on top. Spread the frozen raspberries over it, cover them with the rest of the cream so that they are no longer visible. Spread crumbled speculoos (quantity as desired) over it.

The cream must be kept cold for at least 4 hours.
Before serving, you can sprinkle some powdered sugar over it.

ROASTED ALMONDS WITH LITTLE SUGAR

vegetarian

Total time approx. 15 Minutes

1597 calories

ingredients
200 g almond, whole, unpeeled
50 ml water
50 g sugar
1 package vanilla sugar
½ teaspoon cinnamon
butter, for greasing

preparation
Let a coated pan get hot.
Bring the water to the boil together with sugar, vanilla sugar and cinnamon.
Add the almonds and let it boil further while stirring. The sugar begins to dry and it becomes crumbly. Keep stirring! Until the sugar starts to melt again and pulls threads.

Pour it on a baking tray greased with some butter. Immediately start separating the almonds (I use 2 forks) so that they do not stick together as a lump.

Let them cool down completely on the baking tray.

I wrap the roasted almonds in bags and have a nice, tasty souvenir.

CHRISTMAS TIRAMISU

vegetarian

Total time approx. 30 Minutes

786 calories

ingredients
200 g cream (alternatively cream fines for whipping)
250 g Mascarpone
250 g cream quark or low-fat quark
100 g sugar
1 package vanilla sugar
200 g speculoos (butter or spice speculoos)
400 g berries, mixed

preparation
Whip the cream until stiff. Mix mascarpone, quark, sugar and vanilla sugar and fold in the cream.

In a square casserole dish, spread about 3 tablespoons of the cream, place a layer of Spekulatius on top. Spread the berries on top (the frozen fruits can be taken out of the refrigerator the evening before). Spread the rest of the cream on top and cover with Spekulatius.

Keep in a cool place for 4-5 hours or even overnight until consumed. Dust with powdered sugar before serving.

Tips: I personally prefer to use small crumbled speculoos for the last layer, so that it is easier to scoop the dessert out of the mould later.
Of course, you can also make everything a little less caloric and

replace the cream with Cremefine for whipping (maybe you can even try the vanilla variation) or maybe only use low-fat curd without mascarpone. But then stir the quark a little bit with the mixer before. Stirring for a longer time will make the quark much creamier.

LOW CARB
GINGERBREAD

vegetarian

Working time approx. 20 Minutes
Cooking/baking time approx. 20 Minutes
Total time approx. 40 Minutes

ingredients
180 g hazelnuts, ground
65 g almond, chopped
3 medium sized egg
165 g sweetener, e.g. erythritol or similar
½ Package gingerbread spice
2 g cinnamon powder
1 teaspoon baking soda
80 g chocolate, 85% cocoa content

preparation
For 8-10 pieces.
Mix the ground hazelnuts, chopped almonds and sweetener with the spices. Add the eggs and stir well.

Now form plum-sized balls and put them on a baking tray with baking paper. Press the balls flat on the baking tray.

Put the gingerbread into the oven preheated to 180° C and bake for 20 minutes.

After baking let the gingerbread cool down. Melt the chocolate and spread on the gingerbread.

COCONUT MACAROONS

vegetarian

Working time approx. 15 Minutes
Cooking/baking time approx. 20 Minutes
Total time approx. 35 Minutes

ingredients
200 g grated coconut
1 pack of powdered sugar
1 pack of marzipan paste
2 tablespoons rum
5 egg white
½ Lemon, juice thereof

preparation
Pick the marzipan into small pieces and mix well with the other ingredients. Best with a hand mixer.

Use a spoon to spread small heaps of marzipan on a greased baking tray, not too tight, they will get a bit bigger. Bake at 180 degrees for 20 minutes.

BAKED APPLE CAKE

vegetarian

Working time approx. 40 Minutes
Rest period approx. 1 day
Total time approx. 1 day 40 Minutes

368 calories

ingredients
250 g flour
250 g sugar
1 egg
150 g butter
½ Package baking powder
3 cups of cream, (a 250 g)
1 package vanilla sugar
1 bag pudding powder, vanilla
6 apples

preparation
Knead the flour, half of the sugar, 1 egg, 150 g butter and the baking powder and chill for 30 minutes.
Then put it into a greased springform pan and press it flat, also pull up a rim.
Peel the apples and cut it out with the apple cutter and put it on the bottom of the springform pan.
Bring 2 cups of cream to a boil and use the 3rd cup to mix the pudding powder (incl. rest sugar and vanilla sugar). Boil the pudding and pour it immediately over the apples.
Bake at 175 degrees on the lowest rack for about 70 minutes.

Can be sprinkled with cinnamon and sugar. Afterwards keep cold for 24 hours.

RAISINS - YEAST PLAIT

vegetarian

Working time approx. 30 Minutes
Rest period approx. 2 hours
Total time approx. 2 hours 30 Minutes

ingredients
250 ml milk
1 package yeast, fresh
80 g sugar
500 g wheat flour
1 lemon, untreated, grated peel
½ teaspoon salt
8 tablespoons oil, (germ oil)
150 g raisins
1 egg yolk
hail sugar, for sprinkling
grease, for the sheet metal

preparation
Heat milk lukewarm, dissolve the yeast in it. Add sugar, flour, lemon zest, salt and oil and knead until the dough is separated from the bottom of the bowl. Then knead in the raisins. Let the dough rise in a warm place for approx. 30 min. covered.

Now divide the dough into 3 portions and form rolls of 30 cm each, braid them into a plait. Press the ends firmly, place the plait on a greased baking tray and let it rise again for about 30 minutes.

Now bake the plait in a preheated oven (electric oven: 175°C) for 25 minutes. But 10 minutes before the end of the baking time, sprinkle the plait with beaten egg yolk and sugar.

BUTTER COOKIES

vegetarian

Working time approx. 45 Minutes
Rest period approx. 1 hour
Cooking/baking time approx. 12 Minutes
Total time approx. 1 hour 57 Minutes

5364 calories

ingredients
500 g flour
200 g sugar
1 package vanilla sugar
350 g butter
2 egg yolks
1 egg
some lemon peel, grated
1 pinch of salt
Egg yolk for spreading

preparation
Pour the flour into the bowl and sprinkle the sugar and vanilla sugar over it. Press a hollow in the middle and put the butter in flakes on the rim. Put the egg yolks and the egg into the hollow, add the lemon zest and salt and knead everything quickly with the dough hook or hands to a smooth dough. Put the dough in a closed bowl and refrigerate for at least one hour.

Roll out the dough on a floured surface and cut out shapes (e.g. stars or hearts). Place on a baking tray with baking paper. Spread with egg yolk and decorate according to taste. Bake at 175 °C for 10 - 12 minutes.

SNOWBALLS

vegetarian

Working time approx. 30 Minutes
Cooking/baking time approx. 20 Minutes
Total time approx. 50 Minutes

2960 calories

ingredients
240 g flour
50 g powdered sugar
25 g cornstarch
160 g butter, soft
20 g vanilla sugar
powdered sugar to dust as desired
80 g walnuts

preparation
Put the flour, powdered sugar and starch in a bowl and sieve well. Then chop the walnuts finely with a sharp knife. Then put all ingredients except the walnuts into a bowl and knead to a crumbly dough. Finally, briefly knead the walnuts.

For the cookies, remove some of the dough, press together with your hands and form into small balls of dough. Then place the balls on a baking tray covered with baking paper with some space between them.

Bake in the preheated oven at 160 °C top/bottom heat for about 20 minutes.

Finally, dust the hot snowball cookies with powdered sugar.

This will make them sticky.

The snowball is a delicate short pastry cookie for the Christmas season. The light walnut taste makes them a nice change to the classic Christmas recipes. The powdered sugar cover gives them the snowball look.

Makes 60 pieces.

CINNAMON COOKIE BALLS

vegetarian

Working time approx. 20 Minutes
Cooking/baking time approx. 6 Minutes
Total time approx. 26 Minutes

1997 calories

ingredients
For the dough:
180 g flour
95 g butter
60 g sugar, white
50 g sugar, brown
1 package vanilla sugar
1 medium sized egg
¼ teaspoon salt

Also:
30 g sugar, brown
1 teaspoon cinnamon

preparation
For the dough, mix the butter with salt, white and brown sugar to a creamy, smooth mixture. Add the egg and vanilla sugar and mix in. Weigh the flour and gradually add it, stirring constantly, until you have a tough, sticky dough. (When the bowl is turned over, similar to whipped cream, nothing should fall out!)

Mix brown sugar and cinnamon well in a bowl. Then form small portions of the dough into balls (diameter approx. 4 cm) and roll them in the cinnamon sugar.

Spread the balls with about 10 cm distance on a baking tray covered with baking paper. Bake on the middle rack at 200 °C convection oven for 6 to 8 minutes.

After 6 minutes (recommended) the cookies are very juicy, after 8 minutes they are slightly drier, but better caramelized.

The recipe results in about 30 cookies.

GINGER - HAZELNUT - CUBES

vegetarian

Working time approx. 45 Minutes
Rest period approx. 2 hours
Total time approx. 2 hours 45 Minutes

3240 calories

ingredients
100 g ginger, candied
140 g powdered sugar
175 g butter, cold
250 g flour
70 g hazelnuts, finely chopped
1 small lime
1 pinch of salt

preparation
Cut the ginger into tiny pieces (remove approx. 1 tablespoon for decoration).

Knead the rest of the ginger, 60 g powdered sugar, butter, flour, hazelnuts and a pinch of salt to a smooth dough (using a hand mixer or food processor). On the floured work surface, roll out a rectangle of approx. 15 x 25 cm, approx. 1.5 cm thick, cut through in the middle (for better transport) and covered with cling film for 1 hour, placed in the refrigerator.

Remove foil and cut small cubes (edge length approx. 2 cm).

Place them on a baking tray (baking paper). Refrigerate again for 1/2 hour.

Bake in the oven preheated to 180°, on the 2nd rack from below, for about 15 - 20 minutes (the edge should be nice and light brown). Remove from the oven and let cool down a little.

In the meantime, mix the remaining powdered sugar and approx. 2 tablespoons lime juice to a smooth mixture. Dip the ginger cubes with the upper side slightly into the mixture, let them drip off a little and decorate with the remaining ginger pieces. Dry and let it cool down.

They only really develop their aroma after about 1 week.
In a well closed tin can the cubes will keep for about 4-6 weeks.

SPICE CUTS

vegetarian

Total time approx. 30 Minutes

4612 calories

ingredients
250 g margarine
300 g sugar
1 package vanilla sugar
4 egg
1 package of chocolate pudding powder
2 tablespoons cocoa powder
250 g flour
1 package baking powder
1 package gingerbread spice
125 ml milk
2 tablespoons rum

preparation
Mix all ingredients together without lumps. Place in a greased baking tray or baking frame.

Bake at 180 °C top/bottom heat for about 20 minutes.

CHOCOLATE COOKIES

vegetarian

Total time approx. 20 Minutes

3311 calories

ingredients
175 g flour
1 tablespoon baking powder
125 g butter
150 g sugar
1 egg
200 g dark chocolate

preparation
Makes approx. 20 cookies
Melt the butter and chocolate together in a bain-marie. In the meantime, beat the egg with the sugar until foamy. Then stir in the slightly cooled chocolate-butter mixture, mix flour and baking powder and stir in as well.

Place the dough heaps by the spoonful on a baking tray lined with baking paper and leave enough space between them, as the dough will be quite apart.

Bake the cookies in a preheated oven at 180°C for 10 to 12 minutes. The cookies are still soft then, but when they cool down they will become really firm. Only then put them into tins, otherwise they will crumble. Makes about 20 cookies. They are crispy, but still a bit chocolaty moist.

Always very popular with children, too!

TEA BREAD

vegetarian

Total time approx. 35 Minutes

321 calories

ingredients
6 Egg white
150 g powdered sugar
1 pinch of salt
100 g almonds or nuts, finely grated
30 g candied lemon peel or aranzini, finely chopped
40 g chocolate, grated
50 g flour (wheat flour)
50 g butter, liquid

preparation
Beat the 6 egg whites with half of the sugar and a pinch of salt until stiff, so that a tough, shiny snow is formed. Mix well nuts or almonds, candied lemon peel or aranzini, grated chocolate, flour and the remaining sugar and mingle them with a wooden spoon in the snow. Finally, carefully stir in the lukewarm liquid butter.
The mixture is filled into a buttered and floured rectangular form with a higher rim, 4-5 cm thick and baked at 125-150°C circulating air on a middle rack for 50-55 minutes.

STOLLEN CONFECTIONERY

vegetarian

Working time approx. 2 hours
Rest period approx. 1 hour
Cooking/baking time approx. 15 Minutes
Total time approx. 3 hours 15 Minutes

9501 calories

ingredients
250 g raisins
100 g candied orange peel
75 g almond, chopped
40 ml rum

For the dough: (predough)
500 g flour
2 teaspoons cinnamon
50 g sugar
125 ml milk
1 cube yeast
For the dough: (butter-sugar mass)
200 g butter
125 g powdered sugar
25 g almond, chopped
25 g powdered sugar
2 tablespoons Amaretto
Also:

300 g butter
300 g powdered sugar

preparation

Pour the rum over the raisins, candied orange peel and almonds, cover and allow to infuse.

Sift flour, salt, sugar and spices into a bowl, mix and make a depression in the middle. Pour the milk into this depression and crumble the yeast into it. Stir milk and yeast together gently and cover and leave to rise in a warm place for 15 minutes.

Meanwhile, whisk 200 g butter with 150 g powdered sugar until foamy. Finely grind the almonds with 25 g powdered sugar in a blender and add as much Amaretto as necessary to form a bound mass. Mix this with the butter powdered sugar mass.

First mix the pre-dough with remaining flour, then add the butter-sugar mass and the pickled fruits. Cover the dough and leave to rise for another 30 minutes.

Form the dough into thin rolls and cut them into 2 cm long pieces. Place the confectionery on a baking tray covered with baking paper with a distance of approx. 2 cm and let it rise for another 10 minutes.

Then bake in the preheated oven at 200 °C top/bottom heat for about 15 minutes.

Meanwhile melt 300 g butter. Turn the confectionery pieces while still hot in the liquid butter and then roll them in powdered sugar until they are completely covered.
Let them cool down on cake racks covered with baking paper. Then seal the stollen confectionery in airtight tins and let it stand for at least two weeks.

SNICKERDOODLES

vegetarian

Working time approx. 30 Minutes
Rest period approx. 12 hours
Total time approx. 12 hours 30 Minutes

ingredients
180 g flour
½ Package baking powder
60 g butter
100 g sugar, brown
2 egg
350 g raisins
400 g walnuts, in halves or quarters (= approx. 1 kg with shell)
400 g cherry, candied, quartered or 300-400 g cocktail cherries
125 ml whisky, (Bourbon)
1 ½ Teaspoon cinnamon, ground
¼ teaspoon cloves, ground
¼ teaspoon nutmeg, ground

preparation
Results in approx. 120 pieces
Cover the raisins and soak them in whisky overnight.
Beat butter with sugar and eggs until frothy. Add flour, baking powder and the ground spices (cinnamon, cloves, nutmeg) and work into a smooth dough.
Fold the drained raisins, half the walnut kernels and the cherries into this dough.
Using two teaspoons, place small heaps of dough on a greased baking tray or baking paper.

Bake in a preheated (!) oven at 180 °C for 15 minutes (3rd shelf).

Store in a safe place: Stored in tin cans, they remain softer; they should also freeze very well. But it has never come that far with us, because:

These delicious cookies have been baked in our family tradition for over 25 years and every year they are the absolute hit among the 30 or so types of cookies I bake for Christmas. Family, friends, acquaintances, guests and colleagues are always completely enthusiastic!

CHRISTMAS CAKE

vegetarian

Total time approx. 30 Minutes

8520 calories

ingredients
350 g flour
300 g sugar
150 g candied lemon peel, finely chopped or weighed
100 g hazelnuts, ground
1 package vanilla sugar
1 package baking powder
1 package gingerbread spice
¼ Liters of milk
150 g butter
2 tablespoons honey
4 egg

For the casting:
10 tablespoons of sugar
250 g coconut oil
2 tablespoons cocoa powder
2 egg

preparation
For the dough, mix the ingredients from flour to gingerbread spice dry. Mix the ingredients from milk to eggs as well and mix well with the dry matter.
Spread the dough evenly on a baking tray lined with baking paper and bake in a preheated oven at 170°C on the middle shelf

for approx. 30 minutes.

Turn the finished, still warm cake onto a grid and remove the baking paper.

For the icing, whisk the eggs and sugar until frothy. Heat up the coconut oil. Slowly stir in together with the cocoa powder. Then spread on the cooled cake.

Let the cake stand for one night and then cut it.

ORANGES - CHOCOLATES - COOKIES

vegetarian

Working time approx. 30 Minutes
Rest period approx. 2 hours
Total time approx. 2 hours 30 Minutes

2931 calories

ingredients
200 g flour
60 g cornstarch
1 teaspoon baking powder
100 g sugar
1 package vanilla sugar
1 package of aroma (orange back) or grated peel of an orange
1 egg
125 g butter
100 g dark chocolate

preparation
Mix the flour with cornflour and baking powder, sieve into a mixing bowl. Add sugar, vanilla sugar, orange peel, egg and butter. Mix the ingredients with the hand mixer with dough hook, first briefly at lowest and then at highest speed. Cut the chocolate into small pieces, knead briefly on medium heat, then knead everything on the work surface to a smooth dough.

Form the dough into 3 rolls of about 3 cm thick, press them wide so that the dough strips are about 5 cm wide and a good 1 cm high, chill until the dough has hardened.

Cut the dough strips with a sharp knife into almost 1/2 cm thick slices, place them on a baking tray and bake in the preheated oven at 180°C (top/bottom heat) for about 10 minutes.

HAZELNUT - COOKIES

vegetarian

Total time approx. 25 Minutes

4923 calories

ingredients
200 g butter
220 g sugar, brown
2 egg
1 teaspoon cinnamon
300 g flour
1 pinch of salt
2 teaspoons baking powder
120 g hazelnuts, ground
100 g chocolate flakes

preparation
Results in approx. 50 pieces
Mix butter + sugar until creamy and then fold in the eggs one by one. Mix dry ingredients and then stir in. Place the piles on a baking tray (greased or with baking paper) with two teaspoons - note: the cookies run a little wide! In my case they will fill up about 2 trays, so about 50 pieces.

Bake at about 175°C (preheated) for about 15 minutes.

HAZELNUT - CROISSANT

vegetarian

Total time approx. 30 Minutes

60 calories

ingredients
200 g butter
200 g heavy cream cheese
300 g flour
40 g sugar, brown
40 g sugar
40 g hazelnuts, ground
possibly chocolate coating, dark and white

preparation
Results in 64 croissants
Put butter, cream cheese and flour into a mixing bowl and knead with the dough hooks of the hand mixer to a smooth dough. Wrap in foil and put in the freezer for about 15 minutes. Divide dough into 4 dough pieces. Mix brown and white sugar with the ground hazelnuts. Spread 1/4 on the work surface. Roll out 1 piece of dough on it round (approx. 26cm). Use a cake divider to divide into 16 pieces. (Alternatively, cut into 16 pieces with a knife).

Process remaining dough in the same way. Roll up the pieces to croissants, starting at the broad side and rolling up to the top.

Place the croissants on 2 baking trays lined with baking paper with the tip pointing upwards. Bake the croissants one after the other in the preheated oven (electric: 175 degrees/circulating air 150 degrees) (gas: level 2) for about 12 minutes.

If you like chocolate, you can additionally coat the croissant tips with dark and white couverture.

CHOCOLATE - MINT - COOKIES

vegetarian

Working time approx. 1 hour
Rest period approx. 1 hour
Total time approx. 2 hours

3793 calories

ingredients
1 ½ cup of flour
1 ½ teaspoon baking powder
1 bar of mint-flavoured chocolate (100 g)
1 ½ Chocolate bars (dark chocolate)
6 tablespoons butter
¾ cup of sugar
1 package vanilla sugar
2 egg
powdered sugar to taste

preparation
Mix flour and baking powder in a bowl and put aside.

Melt the mint chocolate and 1 bar of bitter chocolate in a bowl in a water bath or microwave and stir until smooth. Finely chop the remaining half bar of bitter chocolate.

Now beat the butter with the sugar and vanilla sugar until foamy. Stir in the melted chocolate and add the eggs one by one, continuing to beat. Add the flour and baking powder mixture little by little. Finally, stir in the chopped chocolate. The dough is tough, should now have the consistency of a sponge cake and fall heavily from the spoon.

Divide the dough into 2 portions and place each portion on a piece of cling film (no aluminum foil), then press flat in a rectangular shape and wrap. Put the dough in the freezer for about 1 hour until the dough keeps its shape.

Put the powdered sugar in a bowl. Now cut the dough into small cubes and form a small ball from each cube with cold hands. Roll them vigorously in the powdered sugar and place them on a prepared baking tray.

Bake in the preheated oven at 180°C for about 10-12 minutes. The ball should melt, so that the powdered sugar cover bursts open and the cookies look like ice mountains.

CHOCOLATE BREAD

vegetarian

Total time approx. 30 Minutes

ingredients
250 g butter
250 g sugar
6 egg
125 g dark chocolate
125 g chocolate, whole milk
250 g almond, grated
100 g flour
Cake glaze (chocolate)

preparation
Melt dark and milk chocolate over a water bath, make a sponge from the remaining ingredients, add melted chocolate. Spread the dough on a greased baking tray.
Bake at 175°C for about 20-25 minutes, cover with chocolate icing, let cool, cut into cubes or lozenges.

BUTTER BUTTONS

vegetarian

Total time approx. 20 Minutes

3073 calories

ingredients
200 g butter, soft
100 g powdered sugar, sieved
2 packs vanilla sugar
1 egg white
150 g flour
150 g cornstarch
some flour to form

preparation
Mix butter, powdered sugar, vanilla sugar and egg white. Mix flour and starch and sieve, stir 2/3 into the mixture and knead in the rest. If the dough is still too sticky, put it in the fridge for a few minutes.

Form a 1.5 cm thick roll, cut off 1.5 cm thick slices and place them on the baking tray in a round shape. Press it flat with a floured fork so that the notches are clearly visible. Now put the cookies into the not preheated oven and bake at 170°C (hot air) for 8 - 10 minutes.

GINGERBREAD HEARTS

vegetarian

Total time approx. 30 Minutes

ingredients
200 g margarine or butter
250 g sugar
500 g honey
1 package gingerbread spice
4 tablespoons cocoa powder (heaped tablespoons)
2 egg
1 kg flour
½ Package baking powder
1 pinch of salt
almond at will, peeled

preparation
Heat margarine or butter, sugar and honey briefly in a pot. Stir in gingerbread spice and cocoa powder well and let it cool down to room temperature again. Then add eggs, flour, baking powder and salt and knead the dough well.

Roll out the dough about 1/2 cm thick and cut out the hearts (or of course other shapes). Decorate as you like with the peeled almonds.

Bake in a preheated oven at 180°C for about 10-15 minutes (depending on how dark you like them).

Enough for about 40 medium sized hearts.

APPLE SPECULOOS MUFFINS

vegetarian

Working time approx. 15 Minutes
Cooking/baking time approx. 20 Minutes
Total time approx. 35 Minutes

ingredients
200 g flour
1 package baking powder
3 egg
1 package vanilla sugar
150 g sugar
140 ml oil
65 ml milk
1 shot of rum
1 teaspoon cinnamon
8 Speculoos
2 apples

preparation
First sift flour and baking powder into a bowl. Then add the rest of the ingredients except the apples and cookies and mix well. I use the blender for this, but a large spoon will do.

Peel the apples and cut them into small pieces. Crumble the speculoos in a freezer bag. Then fold everything briefly into the dough.

Line the muffin tin with moulds and fill in the dough. I always use 2 tablespoons, that works quite well.

Bake the muffins in the preheated oven at 180 degrees top/bottom heat for 20 - 25 minutes.

BAISER

vegetarian

Working time approx. 20 Minutes
Cooking/baking time approx. 1 hour 30 Minutes
Total time approx. 1 hour 50 Minutes

ingredients
4 egg white, approx. 140 g
200 g sugar, fine
some lemon juice
at will food coloring

preparation
Beat the cold egg white until very stiff, then add a few drops of lemon juice. This gives special stability.
Gradually add half of the sugar, beating vigorously, and continue beating until the mixture is firm. Add the rest of the sugar at once, continue beating vigorously until the mixture is very stiff, smooth and shiny.
Immediately use a piping bag or cake syringe to squirt different shapes onto a baking tray lined with baking paper.

Dry slowly with low heat at 100 - 120 degrees top/bottom heat in a preheated oven for 60 - 90 minutes, depending on size. Do not allow the meringue/meringue rings to brown.

You can also color small amounts with food coloring and spray them onto the baking tray as curls, hearts or pretzels, there are no limits to your imagination. Then garnish with cookies or decorative beads. When they are ready, this is a slightly different but delicious Christmas tree decoration.

RUM BALLS

vegetarian

Working time approx. 20 Minutes
Rest period approx. 2 hours
Total time approx. 2 hours 20 Minutes

ingredients
100 g butter
100 g powdered sugar
200 g whole milk chocolate
100 g chocolate
4 tablespoons rum (54%)
Milk chocolate sprinkles

preparation
100 g of mass results in about 8 pieces, so in total about 40 rum balls.

Stir butter until very foamy, add powdered sugar through a sieve to the butter, melt chocolate in a water bath. Stir the liquid chocolate and rum into the butter-sugar mixture. Let the mixture rest in the refrigerator for about 1 hour.

Dip hands in cold water and form small balls with the help of a spoon. Roll the balls in the chocolate sprinkles. Put them on a plate and put them back in the fridge for about 1 hour.

Pour into small cellophane bags (95 x 160 mm) of 100 g each, bind them with a slip and maybe put a label on them, so you get a small present.

LEBKUCHEN

vegan

Working time approx. 40 Minutes
Rest period approx. 1 Day
Cooking/baking time approx. 15 Minutes
Total time approx. 1 Day 55 Minutes

ingredients
3 tablespoons flax seed, ground (linseed)
140 ml milk, vegetable (rice milk, soy milk)
300 g ground almond
75 g walnuts, roughly chopped
5 Almond (bitter almonds)
60 g candied orange peel
60 g candied lemon peel
1 teaspoon lemon peel
2 teaspoons tartaric baking powder
130 g agave syrup
50 g maple syrup, grade C
50 g sugar, brown
3 teaspoons apricot jam
3 tablespoons gingerbread spice
24 wafers, gluten-free
100 g chocolate coating, black
15 g coconut oil, hard

preparation
Mortar the crushed linseed into flour. Pour this flour into the mixing bowl together with the herbal drink and set aside to swell.

Prepare the solids in a second bowl: Weigh the almond flour, walnuts, candied lemon peel, candied orange peel, baking powder, lemon peel and spices. Wrap the five bitter almonds in some cling film and work them into flour with a hammer. Add the bitter almond flour to the remaining dry ingredients and mix.

Briefly whip the linseed milk with the electric mixer, then stir in the sugar and apricot jam. While continuing to stir, add the solids by the spoonful until everything becomes a sticky brown mass.

Spread two baking papers in sheet size on the trays and place 12 wafers per paper. Put a tablespoon of dough on each wafer.

Prepare a bowl of water and moisten your hands. Form the dough on the wafers flat and smooth, the water will prevent it from sticking. Re-moisten your hands every 1 or 2 gingerbread wafers, but do not flood them, so that the wafers do not soften too much. When all the gingerbreads have a smooth surface, put them in a safe place and let them dry for 24 hours.

The following day, preheat the oven to 160 °C bottom/high and bake the gingerbread for 15 minutes.

After cooling down, chop the chocolate and melt it together with the coconut oil in the microwave or a water bath. Dip the gingerbread into the chocolate, drain and put back on the baking tray so that the coating hardens.

CINNAMON STARS

vegetarian

Working time approx. 30 Minutes
Total time approx. 30 Minutes

2709 calories

ingredients
190 g powdered sugar
100 g almond, ground
200 g nuts, ground
2 egg white
1 teaspoon cinnamon
1 squirt of lemon juice

preparation
Beat the egg white and powdered sugar until stiff. Put 1/3 of it aside and work the rest with the other ingredients (but only 100g nuts), not with a whisk but with a spoon. Finally knead the mixture. Roll out the dough on the remaining nuts to a thickness of about 8-10 mm and cut out stars.
Put them on a baking tray with baking paper and spread generously with the remaining egg white glaze.
Bake at 150°C for approx. 10-12 minutes, after 8 minutes open the oven with a wooden spoon and leave a small gap for the rest of the baking time.

CINNAMON BUNS - BISCUITS

vegetarian

Working time approx. 20 Minutes
Rest period approx. 3 hours
Total time approx. 3 hours 20 Minutes

2254 calories

ingredients
60 g butter, soft
50 g cream cheese
140 g sugar
1 package vanilla sugar
1 egg yolk
180 g flour
1/2 teaspoon baking powder
2 tablespoons butter, liquid
2 teaspoons, heaped cinnamon powder

preparation
For the dough, mix the butter with the cream cheese in a bowl with the whisks of the hand mixer. Stir in 80 g sugar, the vanilla sugar and the egg yolk. Mix flour and baking powder, sieve over the mixture and stir in.

Roll out the dough between two layers of cling film to a rectangle (approx. 20 x 30 cm). Remove the upper cling film. Coat the dough with melted butter, mix the remaining sugar with the cinnamon in a small bowl and generously sprinkle the dough. Set aside about 1 tablespoon of cinnamon sugar on a large plate.

Roll up the dough rectangle with the help of the foil from the narrow side, roll the dough roll all around in the remaining cinnamon sugar, wrap it tightly in the foil and put it in a cool place for 3 hours.

Preheat the oven to 180°C, line a baking tray with paper. Roll out the dough roll, cut it into slices of about 1/2 cm thickness and place them on the baking tray. Bake the cookies on the middle shelf for 12 minutes until light.

Take out the cinnamon rolls and let them cool down on a cake rack.

MACADAMIA - BISCUITS

vegetarian

Total time approx. 30 Minutes

4677 calories

ingredients
200 g chocolate, white
200 g nuts (macadamia nut kernels)
1 vanilla pod
150 g butter
100 g sugar, brown
1 pinch of salt
1 egg
200 g flour
1 teaspoon baking powder

preparation
Finely chop the chocolate and macadamia nuts with a large knife and set aside. Cut the vanilla pod in half lengthwise and scrape out the pulp. Beat the soft fat, brown sugar and vanilla pulp until creamy. Add salt, egg, flour and baking powder and continue stirring. Stir in half of the chocolate-nut mixture.
Using a teaspoon, place small heaps of dough at a distance on trays lined with baking paper and press in some of the chocolate-nut mixture that has been retained. Bake in a preheated oven at 175°C / circulating air 150°C / gas mark 2 for about 12 to 15 minutes.

ALADUSHKI

vegetarian

Total time approx. 30 Minutes

ingredients
Flour as required
2 egg
½ Package baking powder
½ Pack of vanilla sugar
5 tablespoons of sugar
½ Cup of buttermilk
Oil

preparation
Whisk the eggs with a fork. Add vanilla sugar and baking powder and continue beating. Add the buttermilk and stir in the sugar. Stir in enough flour to form a thick dough.

Pour the dough by the spoonful into a pan with hot oil when the underside is lightly browned, turn the aladushki over and finish baking.

Sprinkle it with powdered sugar as desired and enjoy with any compote, jam, honey or maple syrup!

STUFFED POPPY SEED COOKIES

vegetarian

Working time approx. 1 hour 20 Minutes
Cooking/baking time approx. 12 Minutes
Total time approx. 1 hour 32 Minutes

ingredients
250 g butter, soft
125 g powdered sugar
1 package vanilla sugar
4 drops of bitter almond flavor from the tube
1 pinch of salt
300 g flour
1 package of poppy seed bake
150 g jam, red
100 g chocolate coating, white

preparation
Preheat the oven to 180 degrees top and bottom heat.

Put the butter in a bowl and stir with a mixer until smooth. Gradually add sieved powdered sugar, vanilla sugar, aroma and salt while stirring until a bound mass is formed. Stir in sifted flour and poppy seed baking alternately in 2 portions briefly at lowest setting.

Pour the dough in portions into a piping bag with 8 mm perforated spout and splash dab onto the baking tray lined with baking paper. Bake for 10 - 12 minutes. Attention! If you make relatively small dots, check after 7 - 8 minutes so that they do not get too dark!

Pull the pastry with the baking parchment from the baking tray and let it cool down on a cake rack.

For the filling, pass the jam through a sieve. Spread half of the cookies with the jam on the underside, place a second cookie on each and press lightly.

Melt the white couverture in a water bath and dip one side of each cookie in it. Let it set on baking paper.

The recipe makes about 80 cookies.

NOUGAT - COOKIES

vegetarian

Working time approx. 20 Minutes
Rest period approx. 1 hour
Total time approx. 1 hour 20 Minutes

5354 calories

ingredients
200 g butter
75 g sugar
150 g hazelnuts, ground
1 egg
½ teaspoon baking powder
1 package vanilla sugar
250 g flour
400 g chocolate coating

preparation
Make a knead dough from the ingredients (without chocolate coating).
Roll out the dough in small quantities and cut out small round cookies (works best if you put the dough in the fridge beforehand).
Place the cookies on a baking tray covered with baking paper.
Bake at 160°C for about 10 minutes until golden yellow.

Let them cool down on a cake rack.

Dissolve the nougat couverture in a water bath. Put a generous blob on a round cookie and place a second one on top.

Place on a cake rack again until the nougat is dry.

SHORTBREAD COOKIES

vegetarian

Working time approx. 45 Minutes
Cooking/baking time approx. 10 Minutes
Total time approx. 55 Minutes

6814 calories

ingredients
375 g butter or margarine
250 g sugar
2 packs vanilla sugar
1 pinch of salt
375 g flour
125 g cornstarch
125 g hazelnuts, ground, roasted

Also:
100 g sugar, fine
2 teaspoons cinnamon

preparation
Cream butter or margarine. Gradually stir in sugar, vanilla sugar and salt. Mix flour and starch, sieve and stir in 2/3 of the mixture. Knead the dough with the rest of the flour and the ground hazelnuts.

Turn the dough through a mincer with a pastry attachment and place it in wreaths or S-shape on a baking tray covered with baking paper.

Bake in a hot oven at 175 °C - 200 °C top/bottom heat for about 10 minutes (depending on oven).

Dip the half cooled pastry into the sugar mixed with cinnamon.

CINNAMON BALLS

vegetarian

Total time approx. 30 Minutes

3448 calories

ingredients
3 egg white
250 g powdered sugar
1 package vanilla sugar
1 teaspoon cinnamon
300 g hazelnuts, ground
60 g hazelnuts, whole

preparation
Beat egg white until very stiff, gradually add powdered sugar and vanilla sugar and continue beating, set aside about 4 table-spoons of the egg white mixture.

Add cinnamon and mixed nuts to the remaining beaten egg whites.

Shape the mixture into walnut-sized balls and place them on a baking tray, make a small dent with a wooden handle, add some beaten egg white and put 1 hazelnut in each ball.

Preheat oven to approx. 125°C, fan oven to approx. 100°C, bake for approx. 25-30 minutes.

MASCARPONE CREAM WITH CINNAMON STARS

vegetarian

Working time approx. 15 Minutes
Rest period approx. 4 hours
Total time approx. 4 hours 15 Minutes

ingredients
200 g yoghurt (whole milk yoghurt)
200 g quark (low-fat quark)
200 g Mascarpone
2 tablespoons orange juice
1 tablespoon orange liqueur
50 g sugar
1 vanilla sugar
1/2 teaspoon gingerbread spice
16 Cinnamon - Stars
Orange - Zesten

preparation
Mix yoghurt with quark, mascarpone, orange juice, liqueur, sugar, vanilla sugar and gingerbread spice. Crumble 12 cinnamon stars and fill into 4 bowls or glasses. Spread the cream over the crumbs and decorate with the remaining cinnamon stars and orange zest.

CHOCOLATE - WALNUT - BUTTONS

vegetarian

Total time approx. 15 Minutes

ingredients
200 g walnuts, ground or hazelnuts
90 g sugar
100 g chocolate, dark, melted
2 egg white
2 teaspoons Amaretto
½ teaspoon coffee powder, soluble
hazelnuts, or almonds, to decorate

preparation
Dissolve the coffee powder in the Amaretto and mix well with the other ingredients. It becomes a thick, viscous mass.

Form small balls with wet hands and place them on the prepared baking tray, or use a teaspoon to place small piles on the tray. Press one hazelnut or almond each on it, or press something in with a fork.

Bake in a preheated oven at 150° convection oven for about 15 minutes.

Keep the buttons in a closed tin.

Makes approx. 45 pieces..

CHOCOLATE - MARZIPAN CAKE

vegetarian

Total time approx. 20 Minutes

5483 calories

ingredients
400 g marzipan paste
100 g butter
80 g sugar
2 pack vanilla sugar
3 egg
200 g flour
1 package baking powder
1 pinch of salt
60 g chocolate, white
60 g chocolate, whole milk
60 g dark chocolate
20 g flaked almonds
Butter for the mould

preparation
Mix marzipan paste, butter, sugar and vanilla sugar until smooth. Add the eggs bit by bit, stir until smooth. Then add flour, salt and baking powder. Chop the chocolate into pieces of any size and fold into the dough.

Grease a form with butter and sprinkle with almond flakes. Pour in the dough and bake at 160°C (fan oven) for about 35 - 55 minutes.

CHRISTMAS COOKIES

vegetarian

Working time approx. 45 Minutes
Total time approx. 45 Minutes

ingredients
250 g flour
4 teaspoons baking powder
75 g butter
1 package vanilla sugar
4 drops of rum aroma
4 tablespoons of milk
75 g sugar
125 g coconut oil
65 g powdered sugar
25 g cocoa powder
1 package vanilla sugar
1 small bottle of rum aroma
1 egg
75 g almond slivers
400 g chocolate coating

preparation
Knead flour, baking powder, butter, vanilla sugar, sugar, rum aroma and milk into a shortcrust pastry and put it in a cool place. Then roll out the dough, cut out 45 round cookies of about 4 cm diameter and put them on a baking tray.

Put the rest of the dough on the baking tray as well (the shape does not matter) and bake at 175°C for about 10 minutes. Let the cookies cool down and crumble the rest of the dough.

Melt the coconut fat, stir in powdered sugar, cocoa powder, vanilla sugar, egg, almond sticks and the rum aroma. Then fold in the cookie crumbs. Spread the whole thing mountain-like on the baked cookies and cover with melted chocolate coating.

CHOCOLATE ORANGES - KIPFERL

vegetarian

Working time approx. 30 Minutes
Rest period approx. 1 day 6 hours
Total time approx. 1 day 6 hours 30 Minutes

ingredients
125 g butter
1 egg
1 vanilla sugar
100 g sugar
1 teaspoon baking powder
60 g cornstarch
200 g flour
100 g dark chocolate
Orange - peel, rubbed off

preparation
Chop the chocolate with a knife. Mix flour, starch, baking powder, sugar and vanilla sugar in a bowl. Make a depression in the middle. Egg and ger. Orange peel into the deepening. Put butter in flakes on the rim. Spread chocolate on top and knead everything from the middle with the dough hook. Use your hands to knead the chocolate into a smooth dough and put it in the fridge for about 30 minutes. Take the cold dough and form into small croissants (like vanilla croissants). Bake in a preheated oven at 175° C for 15-17 minutes on a baking tray lined with baking paper. Let the crescents cool down and dust with powdered

sugar. For about 30 pieces.

ANGEL'S EYES

vegetarian

Total time approx. 40 Minutes

4044 calories

ingredients
250 g flour
1 teaspoon baking powder
150 g sugar
1 package of vanilla sugar
1 medium sized egg
150 g hazelnuts, ground
1 pinch of salt
125 g butter or margarine
200 g jelly (apricot, quince, elderberry, currant or similar)

preparation
Knead flour, baking powder, sugar, vanilla sugar, egg, hazelnuts, salt and butter (cut into flakes) well. Wrap the dough in cling film and keep cool for about 30 minutes.

Form walnut-sized balls from the dough and press a depression in the middle. Put the cookies on a baking tray covered with baking paper and bake in the preheated oven at 180°C fan oven for approx. 12-15 minutes.

Immediately after baking, press a depression into the cookie with the handle of a wooden spoon, otherwise not enough jelly will fit in. Let cool down.

Now heat up the jelly as required so that it is just liquid. Fill into a freezer bag, cut off one corner and fill the jelly into the depressions of the cookies. Let dry well.

CHOCOLATE SNOWBALLS

vegetarian

Working time approx. 1 hour
Rest period approx. 2 hours
Total time approx. 3 hours

1708 calories

ingredients
100 g chocolate, semi-bitter
50 g butter
60 g powdered sugar
1 teaspoon cinnamon
1 egg
1 egg yolk
¼ teaspoon baking powder
1 tablespoon cocoa powder
100 g flour, sifted
Powdered sugar to roll the snowballs in it

preparation
Melt chocolate with butter in a pot.
Mix all ingredients, including the chocolate and butter mixture, well with a hand mixer and place in a bowl in the refrigerator for at least 2 hours (the dough is very soft, that's right).

Preheat the oven to 170° C. (!) This is important, otherwise the decorative cracks will not appear and they will become a little firmer.

Form walnut-sized balls from the dough and roll them in pow-dered sugar. Put them on a baking tray covered with baking paper.
Bake at 170° C for about 14 minutes.

Store in an airtight tin.

SHORTBREAD COOKIES

vegetarian

Total time approx. 1 hour

ingredients
250 g margarine or butter, soft
200 g powdered sugar
3 packs of vanilla sugar
3 egg yolks
5 tablespoons of milk
1 package of custard powder (vanilla flavor)
380 g flour
chocolate coating, melted

preparation
Enough for about 150 pieces
Mix the soft margarine with the whisks of the hand mixer until creamy. Sift the powdered sugar if necessary and stir in. Add the vanilla sugar and stir in. Add the egg yolks one after the other to the dough and stir each one briefly and only then stir in the milk. Mix flour and pudding powder, sieve over the dough and stir in.

Pour the dough into a piping bag with the desired spout and squirt cookies in any shape onto a baking tray lined with baking paper.

Bake at 200°C (top/bottom heat, fan oven: 180°C) for about 12 minutes. The baking time can vary, as every stove is different. If you try the recipe for the first time, feel free to bake a test tray with a few cookies and see how they turn out.

Dip the cooled cookies into melted chocolate coating.

CHRISTSTOLLEN - GUGELHUPF

vegetarian

Total time approx. 15 Minutes

5950 calories

ingredients
250 g butter, soft
250 g sugar
5 egg
300 g flour
1 lemon, of which the abrasion
1 vanilla pod
1 pinch of salt
150 g raisins
80 g candied orange peel
80 g candied lemon peel
100 g almond slivers
2 cl rum
some powdered sugar

preparation
Cut the vanilla pod open lengthwise and scrape out the pulp. Chop almond sticks roughly. Mix the raisins, candied lemon peel, candied orange peel and the almond sticks with the rum. Beat the soft butter with the sugar until foamy. Gradually add the eggs. Then add the flour, lemon zest, vanilla pulp and salt. Finally fold in the rum mixture.

Butter a cake tin well and fill in the dough. Bake at 180 for about 50 minutes. Make a test with sticks.
To cool down, turn onto a rack and dust with powdered sugar at the end.

CINNAMON WAFERS

vegetarian

Working time approx. 15 Minutes
Rest period approx. 1 Day
Total time approx. 1 Day 15 Minutes

5030 calories

ingredients
250 g butter
250 g sugar
4 egg
500 g flour
40 g cinnamon

preparation
Make the sponge mixture.
Chill for 1 day, bake in portions in a waffle iron.

BUTTER COOKIES

vegetarian

Total time approx. 20 Minutes

ingredients
250 g butter or margarine
200 g sugar, brown
1 package vanilla sugar
375 g flour

preparation
Make a kneading dough from soft fat, sugar, vanilla sugar and flour first with the dough hooks of the hand mixer, then with your hands. Form rolls from the dough (approx. 2 cm) and chill for some time. Cut the rolls into about 5 mm thick slices and put them on a greased or with baking paper covered baking tray.

Baking: approx. 10 - 12 min at 200° C

An ingenious recipe for all those who (not only) like it to be supi simple, quick & above all delicious during the Advent season! Makes about 80 cookies.

OATMEAL COOKIES

vegetarian

Working time approx. 30 Minutes
Cooking/baking time approx. 15 Minutes
Total time approx. 45 Minutes

96 calories

ingredients
500 g oat flakes, seedy
250 g butter
200 g sugar
1 package vanilla sugar
2 egg
1 teaspoon baking powder
50 g flour

preparation
If the oat flakes are particularly large, crumble them slightly with your hands beforehand. Heat butter and pour over the oat flakes, stir well.

In the meantime, stir the eggs with sugar and vanilla sugar until foamy. Together with flour and baking powder pour over the oat flakes and mix everything with a spoon.

Put small heaps of the mixture on the baking tray with two spoons and bake at 180 - 190 °C for about 15 minutes. The cookies should still be light yellow and soft. Remove them from the baking tray immediately, best with a pan knife.

Note about the eggs: either 2 large or 3 small/medium. If necessary, use a little more flour. There must be a homogeneous mass, the mass must not run away from the oat flakes.

Makes about 50 cookies.

SPRINGERLE

vegetarian

Working time approx. 1 hour
Rest period approx. 1 Day
Cooking/baking time approx. 30 Minutes
Total time approx. 1 Day 1 hour 30 Minutes

2274 calories

ingredients
2 large eggs, thick (class L)
250 g powdered sugar
¼ Teaspoon baking soda (1/2 tablet or approx. 0.5 g)
250 g flour (gluten-free flour also possible)
cherry brandy
Bold
Aniseed, whole grains

preparation
Beat the sugar and eggs for at least 45 minutes until fluffy. In the meantime, dissolve baking soda in 1/2 teaspoon of cherry brandy and add to the egg foam, then knead the flour well (the dough must be kneaded for at least 15 minutes). Put the dough into a bowl covered with a cloth soaked in cherry brandy. But it must not be dripping wet! Then cover the bowl with a suitable lid. Important: Do not use a tight-closing bowl (such as a yeast dough bowl)!
Now the dough must rest overnight in a cool place, but not in the refrigerator.

The next day 2 baking trays are greased and sparingly sprinkled with aniseed. Then knead the dough again until it is soft. Now it must not lose its shape; if necessary, some more flour must be kneaded in. But be careful: not too much!

Roll out the dough to a finger thickness on plenty of flour and brush the surface with some flour. Use a Springerle model to shape the surface, cut out the cookies with a dough wheel and place them on the greased baking tray, quietly quite dense, they won't melt during baking.

The cookies have to be kept in the cooler for one night without a cover.

The next day, they are baked in a hot air oven at 140 ° in 30 minutes until they are light yellow.

Springerle are only soft after baking and must become very hard afterwards. They taste best dipped in coffee or tea.

Makes about 30 pieces.

LEBKUCHEN - MUFFINS

vegetarian

Total time approx. 15 Minutes

ingredients
125 g margarine
60 g honey
120 g sugar
2 egg
300 g flour
1 package gingerbread spice
200 ml milk
2 tablespoons cocoa powder
2 teaspoons baking powder
cake glaze, (chocolate glaze)

preparation
Cream the margarine with sugar, honey and the eggs. Sift the flour and mix with the baking powder, cocoa and gingerbread spice. Alternately add some flour and milk to the dough until there is nothing left.

Fill the muffin cups with the dough and bake the tartlets at 200 degrees (preheated) for about 15 minutes.

Cover with chocolate icing.

GINGER COOKIES WITH CHOCOLATE ICING

vegetarian

Working time approx. 40 Minutes
Cooking/baking time approx. 10 Minutes
Total time approx. 50 Minutes

ingredients
For the short pastry:
200 g flour
1/2 teaspoon baking powder
100 g sugar
1 package vanilla sugar
150 g butter, or margarine, soft
2 teaspoons ginger powder, or fresher
1 pinch of salt
50 g ginger root, candied, chopped into fine pieces

For the glaze:
as desired couverture, or chocolate

preparation
Use the dough hook to work all the dough ingredients into a smooth dough. It may be necessary to chill for a while, but this is also possible.
Preheat the oven to 180°C.
Form about 60 small balls and flatten them crosswise with a

fork. Dip fork in flour if necessary. Bake for about 10 minutes.
After cooling, cover with chocolate coating, e.g. dip the cookies
halfway.
Store in a cookie tin.

WHITE MULLED WINE

vegetarian

Total time approx. 10 minutes

ingredients
500 ml white wine
300 ml apple juice, clearer
1 package of aroma (lemon peel, grated)
1 teaspoon ginger powder
75 g rock candy, white
50 ml orange liqueur

preparation
Put white wine, apple juice, lemon peel flavor, ginger and candy together in a pot and bring everything to the boil once. Stir in orange liqueur.

Serve the finished mulled wine hot, e.g. in a teapot or heat-resistant glasses.

PEANUT COOKIES

vegetarian

Total time approx. 30 minutes

96 calories

ingredients
80 g peanuts, unsalted
100 g butter, soft
70 g peanut butter
100 g cane sugar
1 egg
120 g flour
1 teaspoon baking powder
50 g chocolate, dark chocolate

preparation
Coarsely chop peanuts. Mix butter, peanut butter, cane sugar and egg until creamy. Mix flour and baking powder and stir in. Fold in 40 g peanuts.

Place the dough with a teaspoonful of piles on a baking tray covered with baking paper, leaving enough space because the cookies are coming apart. Sprinkle with the remaining peanuts, press down slightly and bake at 160°C (circulating air) for approx. 15 minutes. Carefully loosen and let cool down on a cake wire.

Coarsely chop the chocolate, melt in a bain-marie, fill into a small piping bag and cover the cookies with it in strips. If the cookies are for Christmas, you can decorate them with colorful sugar beads etc.

EGG LIQUEUR - NUT COINS

vegetarian

Total time approx. 20 Minutes

ingredients
300 g flour
200 g butter
100 g powdered sugar
1 package of vanilla sugar
1 egg yolk
170 g walnuts, halved
For the glaze:
3 tablespoons advocaat
75 g powdered sugar

preparation
Cream butter, sugar, vanillin sugar and the egg yolk. Chop the walnuts with a knife or food processor. Knead the flour and 100 g of the chopped walnuts into the butter mixture.

Form three rolls with a length of approx. 20 cm from the dough. Roll the dough rolls in the remaining walnuts, wrap them in aluminium foil and let them freeze slightly in the freezer for 30 minutes. In the meantime, preheat the oven to 180 degrees (hot air).

Then remove the aluminum foil and cut the dough rolls into approx. 1 cm thick slices and place them on a baking tray covered with baking paper and bake for 15 minutes.

For the icing, sieve the powdered sugar and mix it with the advocaat to an even mass. Spread the icing with a cake brush on the cooled down talers and let it dry.

Results in about 60 pieces

PEANUT - COOKIES

vegetarian

Total time approx. 15 Minutes

ingredients
75 g butter
200 g sugar
1 package vanilla sugar
5 drops of butter-vanilla flavor
1 medium sized egg
125 g wheat flour, 405
1 teaspoon baking powder
200 g peanuts, salted, chopped
possibly peanuts, unsalted for garnishing

preparation
Stir the butter with a hand mixer or in a food processor until smooth, add sugar, vanilla sugar and flavoring and stir until a bound mass is formed. Then stir in the egg for 1/2 minute on the highest setting. Then stir in flour, baking powder and peanuts.

Using two teaspoons, place walnut-sized heaps of dough on a baking tray lined with baking paper. Place 1 peanut on each heap as desired. Put the baking tray on the middle shelf into the oven preheated to 180°C (hot air: 160°C) and bake the cookies for about 10 minutes.

MULLED WINE SPICE CAKE WITH CHOCOLATE

vegetarian

Working time approx. 30 Minutes
Rest period approx. 2 hours
Cooking/baking time approx. 1 Stunde
Total time approx. 3 hours 30 Minutes 4375 calories

ingredients
For the dough:
300 g flour
1 package baking powder
150 g sugar
30 g baking cocoa
2 teaspoons cinnamon
1 teaspoon gingerbread spice
nutmeg at will
160 ml milk
200 ml mulled wine, alternatively 160 ml milk
1 egg
150 ml vegetable oil
salt to taste
50 g chocolate drops, ready to bake
For the pouring: (mulled wine)
75 g powdered sugar, sieved
mulled wine at will

For the icing: (sugar-cinnamon)
75 g powdered sugar, sieved
½ teaspoon cinnamon powder
milk to taste

preparation
For the dough mix flour, baking powder, sugar, baking cocoa, cinnamon, gingerbread spice and nutmeg with a tablespoon. Then put milk, mulled wine, egg, vegetable oil and the salt into a mixing bowl and mix. Add the mixture of the dry ingredients spoon by spoon at a low stirring speed until a smooth dough is obtained. Finally, fold the chocolate drops into the dough with a dough scraper.

Preheat the oven to 175 °C top/bottom heat. Grease the cake tin with baking release spray. Alternatively, use a medium-sized box mould. Pour the dough into the tin and bake for about 60 minutes. Check the baking progress with the stick test. After baking, turn over the mulled wine cake while still slightly luke-warm. It must then cool down completely before the icing can be added to the cake.

For the mulled wine icing, sieve the powdered sugar and mix with the mulled wine until a viscous mass is formed. Gradually add the mulled wine until the correct consistency is achieved. If the mass is too liquid, simply mix in some powdered sugar again. Spread the icing on the cake.

Make the beige cinnamon icing just like the reddish mulled wine icing and put it on the cake. If you do not like cinnamon, leave it out.

CINNAMON BROWNIES

vegetarian

Working time approx. 30 Minutes
Cooking/baking time approx. 35 Minutes
Total time approx. 1 hour 5 Minutes

5767 calories

ingredients
For the dough:
200 g dark chocolate (as much cocoa as possible!)
200 g butter
4 egg
250 g sugar
1 teaspoon cinnamon
160 g flour
30 g cocoa powder, unsweetened
For the freezing:
3 tablespoons of butter
3 tablespoons cocoa powder
1 package of vanilla sugar
125 g powdered sugar
1 tablespoon of milk

preparation
For the dough melt butter and chocolate in a bain-marie and let
it cool down a little. Whip the eggs with the sugar until creamy

and then beat in the lukewarm (not hot!) chocolate. Mix the flour with cinnamon and cocoa and stir in.

Fill the dough into a rectangular form of approx. 30 x 20 cm lined with baking paper (can be bigger, give some flat brownies) and bake at 180 °C top/bottom heat for 30 - 35 min.

The dough seems to rise a lot at first, but collapses again after baking - this is how it should be. They should have a light crust on the outside and still be somewhat liquid on the inside.
Leave to cool completely in the form.

Meanwhile, whip the butter with the cocoa until foamy, then add the sieved powdered sugar, vanillin sugar and milk and whip again until creamy.
Turn the cake over, carefully peel off the baking parchment and generously spread the frosting.
Then cut into about 15 small pieces, more if you like.

NOUGAT RODS

vegetarian

Total time approx. 30 Minutes

ingredients
225 g butter
100 g powdered sugar, sieved
1 package vanilla sugar
3 egg yolks
1 teaspoon cinnamon, ground
200 g flour (wheat flour)
40 g cocoa powder
1 teaspoon, heaped baking powder
125 g hazelnuts, kernels, ground, roasted
Nutella
Cake glaze (chocolate)

preparation
Mix butter, powdered sugar, vanilla sugar and egg yolk until smooth. Then gradually stir in cinnamon, wheat flour, cocoa, baking powder and hazelnut kernels. Using a piping bag or similar, press approx. 10 cm strips onto the baking tray and bake at 175 degrees (fan oven) for 7-10 minutes.
Let cool down afterwards. Always glue 2 of them together with Nutella on the bottom and dip them into the warmed chocolate icing on the right and left.

CASHEW-TOFFEES

vegetarian

Working time approx. 15 Minutes
Cooking/baking time approx. 40 Minutes
Total time approx. 55 Minutes

3779 calories

ingredients
For the dough:
150 g butter
1 egg
80g sugar, brown
1 teaspoon vanilla extract
200 g flour
1 pinch of salt

For the flooring:
25 g butter
45 g sugar, brown
450 g condensed milk, sweetened
1 teaspoon vanilla extract
100 g cashew nuts, salted

preparation
Preheat the oven to 180° top/bottom heat (circulating air 150°, gas level 3).

Dough:
Stir the soft butter until smooth. Stir in egg, sugar, 1 pinch of salt and vanilla extract. Fold in the flour and knead to a smooth

dough.

Press the dough into a baking tin (22 x 22 cm) lined with baking paper with a high rim. (Divide larger moulds with aluminium foil folded several times).

Bake on the middle shelf for 20 to 25 minutes.

Topping:

Bring butter, sugar, vanilla extract, a pinch of salt and the condensed milk to the boil in a small saucepan while stirring and let it thicken for about 5 minutes. Then stir in the chopped cashew nuts.

Spread the mixture evenly on the pre-baked dough and bake for another 12 to 15 minutes at the same temperature.

Let the toffees cool down in the tin, then cut into approx. 60 cubes.

EGGNOG - STARS

vegetarian

Working time approx. 1 hour 10 Minutes
Rest period approx. 1 hour
Total time approx. 2 hours 10 Minutes

3865 calories

ingredients
For the dough:
210 g flour, smooth
1/2 teaspoon baking powder
80 g powdered sugar
1 ½ Pack of vanilla sugar
30 ml advocaat
2 egg yolks
100 g butter, (room temperature)

For the filling:
300 ml milk
1 package pudding powder, vanilla, 30 - 40g
60 g sugar, crystal sugar
120 ml advocaat
120 g butter, (room temperature)

preparation
Dough ingredients for about 30 pieces, but the filling is enough
for double the amount. So: either make 2x dough or use the pudding in another way!

Mix flour and baking powder (or sieve), add the remaining ingredients and knead well. Let the dough rest in the fridge for about 30 minutes.

In the meantime prepare the filling:
Mix 100 ml (1/3) of the milk with the pudding powder until smooth, bring the rest of the milk and sugar to the boil. Slowly stir in the pudding and boil it down until a thick mass is formed. Stir in the advocaat and butter, if necessary, using a hand blender or whisk to prevent lumps from forming. Remove from the heat and let it cool down while stirring occasionally. Stir again and, covered with foil, let it cool down completely.

Take the dough out of the fridge, roll out about 3 mm thick and cut out cookies, half of them with a hole in the middle (use thimble if necessary). Place on the baking tray lined with baking paper and bake in the oven preheated to 180° for about 10 minutes (should not brown). After removing the cookies from the oven, carefully pull them off the tray with the baking paper to prevent them from browning (they should remain yellow) and let them cool down.

Cream the cooled eggnog cream and spread it thickly on the underside of the cookies. Place the perforated cookies on top and gently press them together. Finally, place a blob of the remaining cream on the holes and sprinkle with powdered sugar (mixed with the remaining vanilla sugar) if necessary.

RED WINE CAKE

vegetarian

Total time approx. 15 Minutes

542 calories

ingredients
300 g butter
300 g sugar
300 g flour
1 package baking powder
6 egg
⅛ Liters of wine, red
1 teaspoon cinnamon
1 tablespoon cocoa powder
100 g chocolate, dark, grated

For the casting:
200 g powdered sugar
Wine, red
Water, hot

preparation
Beat the soft butter until fluffy. Add sugar, then the eggs. Mix flour with baking powder and stir into the dough together with the remaining ingredients. Finally, fold in the grated chocolate. Pour into a greased and crumbled cake tin and bake at 175° for about 45-50 minutes. Turn out the cake and let it cool down.
For the icing, mix powdered sugar with the red wine and water (in equal parts), so that a viscous mass is formed. Cover the cake with it.

The cake will keep for a whole week and gets better every day, so you can bake it 1-2 days before and put it in a cool place.

SHAKING-LEBKUCHEN

vegetarian

Total time approx. 10 Minutes

839 calories

ingredients
350 g flour
300 g sugar
150 g fruits, chopped, candied
100 g hazelnuts, ground
3 teaspoons gingerbread spice
1 teaspoon clove, ground
1 tablespoon vanilla sugar
1 package baking powder
250 ml milk
150 g butter, liquid
2 tablespoons honey
4 eggs

preparation
Put the dry ingredients into a large mixing bowl, close it and shake vigorously. Then shake the liquid ingredients vigorously in another mixing bowl. Add the liquid ingredients to the dry ingredients and shake vigorously. Stir with the dough scraper and spread on a baking tray. Bake at 200 degrees for about 20 minutes.

After baking, coat with glaze and cut into squares, rectangles or triangles while still warm.

Lemon glaze: Mix 250 g powdered sugar with 2 tablespoons

lemon juice and 2 tablespoons water.

NUT WREATH WITH SHORT PASTRY

vegetarian

Total time approx. 30 Minutes

ingredients
300 g flour
2 teaspoons baking powder
100 g sugar
1 package vanilla sugar
1 egg
2 tablespoons of milk
125 g butter

For the filling:
200 g hazelnuts, ground
100 g sugar
4 drops of bitter almond aroma
½ Egg yolk
1 egg white
8 tablespoons of water

preparation
First knead the ingredients for the dough and chill as a ball (short pastry). Then roll out as a rectangle; be careful, the dough is sticky. Mix the ingredients for the filling and spread it on the short pastry, roll it up and put it in a wreath. Spread with the remaining 1/2 egg yolk and some milk and cut a few times.

Bake at 175-200 degrees for 45 minutes.

Tastes deliciously crispy like cookies - something different and not dry at all. I got the recipe from a good friend and would like to share it with others. Fits well in the cold season and at Christmas.

NUTELLA COOKIES

vegetarian

Total time approx. 30 Minutes

2802 calories

ingredients
185 g flour
60 g cocoa powder
125 g sugar
60 g hazelnuts or almonds, ground or grated coconut
1 egg
1 tablespoon of water
at will Nutella
100 g butter, soft
Flour for the work surface

preparation
Cut the butter into flakes and mix with flour, cocoa, sugar and the ground hazelnuts until crumbly. Add the egg and water to moisten, mix briefly and knead the dough on a floured work surface until smooth.

Roll out the dough on a sheet of baking paper and cut the edges straight. Spread the rolled out dough with Nutella. Then form the dough into a roll. To do this, it is best to lift the baking paper on one side and start rolling it in from there.

Wrap the roll of dough firmly in cling film and put it in the fridge for half an hour to allow the Nutella to set a little. Meanwhile, preheat the oven to 180°C (fan oven). After the resting time, cut the dough roll into slices of about 1 cm thickness and lay them out on a baking tray (with paper) at a sufficient distance (1 - 2 cm).

I always leave the cookies in the oven for only 8 - 10 minutes. Then they still look very soft when you take them out, but after you let them cool down on a cake rack, they have a wonderful consistency, like brownies. If you want crispier cookies, you should take them out of the oven after 12 minutes baking time at the latest.

WALNUT COINS

vegetarian

Total time approx. 20 Minutes

4337 calories

ingredients
250 g flour
250 g butter, soft
125 g powdered sugar
1 package vanilla sugar
1 package of pudding powder, chocolate
1 tablespoon cocoa powder
1 pinch of salt
100 g walnuts, roughly chopped
40 g chocolate flakes

preparation
Mix flour with cocoa powder and pudding powder, add the remaining ingredients and knead everything into a smooth dough.

Divide the dough into 4 parts and form them into rolls, wrap the rolls in cling film and put them in the freezer for about 30 minutes.

Cut the dough rolls with a knife into approx. ½ cm thick slices, put them on a baking tray covered with baking paper and bake at 160 degrees convection oven for 12 - 15 minutes.

Tip: If you like, you can melt some more chocolate and sprinkle it on the cooled cookies.

MARZIPAN CUSTARD

vegetarian

Working time approx. 15 Minutes
Rest period approx. 2 hours
Cooking/baking time approx. 15 Minutes
Total time approx. 2 hours 30 Minutes

6308 calories

ingredients
450 ml milk
200 g marzipan paste
50 ml Amaretto
2 tablespoons of sugar
1 package vanilla sugar
2 tablespoons cornstarch
1 egg

preparation
Put the milk (up to about 5 tablespoons) with the sugar and
vanilla sugar in a pot. Cut the marzipan paste into small pieces
and add them. Heat everything until the marzipan is dissolved,
then bring the milk to the boil.

Mix the 5 tablespoons of milk with the starch and the egg yolk
and add to the boiling marzipan milk. Simmer for another 1
minute while stirring constantly. Remove from the heat and
mix in the Amaretto.

Cover the pudding and chill it (1-2 hours).

Beat the egg white to snow and fold into the cold pudding mixture.

Serve with cinnamon plums and caramelized almonds.

NOUGAT - CURD STOLLEN

vegetarian

Total time approx. 30 Minutes

ingredients
500 g flour
200 g sugar
250 g quark
200 g butter
50 g ground almond
2 egg
2 packs vanilla sugar
1 package baking powder
some lemon peel, grated
1 pinch of salt
flavour to taste, (bitter almond flavour)
150 g nougat, (piece)
100 g butter, melted
Powdered sugar

preparation
Knead a dough from all ingredients except the nougat.
Cut the nougat into cubes (approx. 5x5 mm) and knead quickly into the dough. This should be done quickly, as it becomes slightly soft and melts.

Form a stollen and bake at 175°C for about 45 minutes. If necessary, the baking time can be shorter - make sure to test with sticks!

After cooling down, brush with melted butter and sprinkle with powdered sugar.

This Stollen does not need any storage time and should be eaten as fresh as possible! If you like, you can also add roughly chopped dark chocolate to the dough.

ROUND PEPPER NUTS

vegetarian

Total time approx. 40 Minutes

ingredients
500 g honey
300 g sugar
3 pieces egg
15 g salt of hartshorn
1 teaspoon cinnamon, ground
1 teaspoon cloves, ground
1/2 teaspoon nutmeg
1/2 teaspoon coriander, ground
1/2 teaspoon ginger powder
1/2 teaspoon allspice, ground
1/2 teaspoon cardamom, ground
1 teaspoon, heaped pepper, white
1 kg flour
butter or margarine for the baking tray

preparation
Allow the honey to thicken over a mild heat. Mix the sugar, eggs, salt and all spices well with the honey. Stir in the sifted flour one by one, later knead in.
Preheat the oven to 150 degrees top and bottom heat.

Form small balls of about 2 cm diameter from the dough and place them on the greased baking tray with enough space between them. Bake the pepper nuts on the middle slide bar for 15 - 20 minutes until they are golden yellow. Let them cool down on a cake rack.

Mix powdered sugar with water and coat the pepper nuts with the icing.

LEBKUCHEN BROWNIES

vegetarian

Working time approx. 15 Minutes
Cooking/baking time approx. 40 Minutes
Total time approx. 55 Minutes

10710 calories

ingredients
400 g couverture (whole milk couverture)
400 g butter
200 g hazelnuts, ground
200 g hazelnuts, chopped
300 g sugar, brown
15 g gingerbread spice
1 package baking powder
8 egg
2 packs vanilla sugar
2 pinches of salt
Grease for the mould
For the glaze:
200 g couverture (whole milk couverture)
60 g butter

preparation
Melt 400 g chocolate coating with butter. Mix the hazelnuts with baking powder and add sugar, salt, gingerbread spice and eggs. Add the butter couverture mixture and mix everything

well.

Grease a large rectangular springform pan. Pour in the dough and bake at 160°C for about 40 minutes. Let it cool down a little bit and take it out of the tin.

For the glaze, melt the remaining couverture with 60 g butter and mix well. Pour the glaze onto the still warm cake and let it set.

Cut into rectangles and serve.

FIG SPIRALS

vegetarian

Working time approx. 40 Minutes
Rest period approx. 1 Day
Cooking/baking time approx. 10 Minutes
Total time approx. 1 Day 50 Minutes

3081 calories

ingredients
For the filling:
100 g fig, dried
1 egg
50 g sugar
1 teaspoon of cocoa powder
½ teaspoon cinnamon powder
50 g ground almond
1 tablespoon of rum

For the dough:
250 g wheat flour
100 g sugar
1 package of vanilla sugar
1 egg
125 g butter
Also:
Water
20 g sugar
½ teaspoon cinnamon powder

preparation

Filling:
Cut figs very finely and mix with the other ingredients.

Knead dough:
Sift flour into a bowl. Add the remaining ingredients and mix everything with a hand mixer (dough hook), first at the lowest and then at the highest setting to form a dough.

Roll out the dough to a rectangle of 40 x 20 cm on a lightly floured work surface.
Spread the dough with the fig mixture, leaving 1 cm of edge free. Cut the rectangle in half to make 2 squares of 20 x 20 cm. Roll up both squares tightly, brush all around with water. Mix cinnamon and sugar, roll the rolls in it and put them on a plate. Cover both rolls and put them in a cool place overnight.

Preheat the oven the next day. Cover baking tray with baking paper. Cut the rolls evenly into approx. 1/2 cm thick slices, place them on the baking tray and bake.

Upper/lower heat: approx. 200 °C
Hot air: approx. 180 °C
Gas: Stage 3-4
Baking time: approx. 8-10 minutes
Enough for about 80 pieces

WHITE MOUSSE AU CHOCOLAT

vegetarian

Working time approx. 30 Minutes
Rest period approx. 3 hours
Total time approx. 3 hours 30 Minutes

286 calories

ingredients
3 sheets gelatine, white
150 g chocolate coating, white
3 egg
40 g sugar
1 package of vanilla sugar
2 tablespoons rum, white
200 g whipped cream
1 pinch of cinnamon

preparation
Soak gelatine in cold water. Melt the chocolate coating in a water bath. Separate eggs.
Beat egg yolks, sugar and vanilla sugar until frothy. Add couverture and rum and stir in.
Squeeze the gelatine, dissolve it in a small pot and stir into the egg yolk mixture. Stir in the cinnamon. Let it cool down a little bit.
Whip cream and egg white separately until stiff. Fold the cream first and then the egg white into the chocolate-yolk mixture.

Pour into a bowl and refrigerate for at least 3 hours.
If you don't like cinnamon or if that's too Christmassy for you,
just leave the cinnamon out or replace it with the scraped out
pulp of a vanilla pod. But even without both, the mousse tastes
great. I love to eat warm port plums with it.

PEANUT - CARAMEL - MACARONS

vegetarian

Total time approx. 30 Minutes

65 calories

ingredients
2 egg white
100 g cane sugar
50 g peanut butter, with pieces
150 g peanuts, roasted and salted
25 wafers
1 pinch of salt

preparation
Roughly chop the roasted and salted peanuts. Preheat the oven to 160°C top/bottom heat.

Beat the egg white with a pinch of salt until very stiff. Gradually add the cane sugar while beating constantly. Then fold in the peanut butter and the chopped peanuts.

Place the baking wafers on a baking tray and use 2 teaspoons to place small heaps of the dough on top.

Bake for about 20-25 minutes. Then take them out and let them cool down on a grid.

Makes about 25 pieces.

STUFFED ORANGE COOKIES

vegetarian

Working time approx. 40 Minutes
Rest period approx. 1 hour
Total time approx. 1 hour 40 Minutes

3938 calories

ingredients
160 g butter, soft
160 g powdered sugar
1 package vanilla sugar
1 package of aroma, orange peel aroma (Finessa)
1 bottle aroma - oil, orange flavor
1 large egg
350 g wheat flour, smooth (Type 480)
½ teaspoon baking powder
80 g jelly, orange or marmalade
125 g chocolate coating, whole milk

preparation
The amount is enough for about 60 cookies.
Mix the first 6 ingredients with a mixer until creamy, add flour and baking powder and knead. Put them in cling film and let them rest in the fridge for about 1 hour.

Roll out the dough in 2 portions on floured baking paper about 3 mm thick - also cover the dough with baking paper.
Cut out cookies with a small round cookie cutter, approx. 3 to

3.5 cm, and place them on a baking tray covered with baking paper.

Bake in the oven preheated to 175° top/bottom heat for approx. 12 minutes - please check, they should only be very lightly browned (brown on the hot baking tray as well!)

If you want it to be quick and the appearance is not so important, you can also form the dough into rolls of about 2.5 cm thickness and cut off slices of about 3 mm and bake them like this - but then keep a little more distance, they will run a little bit apart - but they won't get thinner.

I always process the dough leftovers this way.

Put the cooled cookies together with some orange jelly or jam (I like to stir some orange flavor oil into it, you can also branch off the dough). Melt the chocolate coating carefully in a warm water bath and spread a thin layer of cookies on one side.

ICE CONFECTIONERY

vegetarian

Working time approx. 30 Minutes
Rest period approx. 3 hours
Total time approx. 3 hours 30 Minutes

43 calories

ingredients
300 g chocolate coating, semi-bitter
40 g palm fat
40 g butter
30 g coffee powder (cappuccino powder)
100 ml whipped cream

preparation
Melt the chocolate coating, butter, coconut oil and cappuccino powder in the cream in a bain-marie, stir until smooth and pour into a mixing bowl.
Chill until the mixture is almost firm. Then whip with a hand mixer for about 5 minutes until creamy.
Pour into a piping bag with star-shaped spout, squirt into small aluminium sleeves and chill.
Serve chilled. Enough for about 50 pieces.

ANISEED COOKIES

vegetarian

Working time approx. 45 Minutes
Rest period approx. 12 hours
Total time approx. 12 hours 45 Minutes

1313 calories

ingredients
2 egg
150 g powdered sugar
1 teaspoon aniseed, ground
150 g flour

preparation
Beat the eggs and the powdered sugar with the whisk of the food processor to a light cream. Add the aniseed and little by little the flour. Stir for at least 45 minutes in total!

The mixture is then almost white, very viscous and of honey-like consistency. This should help the formation of the feet.

Without a food processor, it is sufficient to beat with the electric hand mixer for about 10 minutes. Line the baking tray with baking paper, butter it and dust it with flour. Use a teaspoon or a piping nozzle to place small heaps on the baking tray. They should flow smoothly on the surface, but not on the baking tray. Dry overnight at room temperature and allow a skin to draw.

Bake the aniseed cookies in a preheated oven at 150°C for about 15 minutes. Ideally, the cookies should have a foamy white cap on a stocky base.

SPAGHETTI BISCUITS

vegetarian

Total time approx. 35 Minutes

ingredients
130 g butter
60 g powdered sugar
1 egg
190 g flour
1 package pudding powder, vanilla
jam, at will
Powdered sugar

preparation
Cream soft butter with powdered sugar and egg, then mix in the flour and pudding powder and knead to a dough - this can be processed immediately - roll out the dough on a well floured board (approx. 3-4 mm thick) and cut out rings (5 cm diameter) - place these on a baking tray covered with baking paper, 1 tsp. of jam on each.

Form balls of approx. walnut size from the dough remains and press them directly onto the jam using the garlic press (cut off the dough with a knife) - bake in the preheated oven at 160° convection oven for approx. 10-12 min - when cold, sprinkle with powdered sugar.

VANILLA - BITS

vegetarian

Working time approx. 30 Minutes
Rest period approx. 2 hours
Total time approx. 2 hours 30 Minutes

4016 calories

ingredients
300 g flour
100 g powdered sugar
200 g butter
50 g ground almond
50 g hazelnuts, ground
2 eggs of which the egg yolk
1 pinch of salt
2 pack vanilla sugar (Bourbon vanilla sugar)
1 package of aroma, (Bourbon vanilla, liquid)
2 packs vanilla sugar (Bourbon vanilla sugar), to roll
½ Cup of powdered sugar, to roll

preparation
Knead the ingredients for the dough into a smooth dough, form
into rolls (3 cm diameter) and wrap in cling film.
Cut the rolls into 0.4 cm thick slices and bake in the preheated
oven on the middle shelf at 190° for 10 - 12 minutes.
Mix half a cup of powdered sugar and 2 packets of bourbon vanilla sugar and roll the still warm taler in it. To allow the vanilla
aroma to develop fully, let the thalers steep for a few days.

NUT BAGS

vegetarian

Total time approx. 30 Minutes

6942 calories

ingredients
300 g flour
225 g hazelnuts, ground
125 g sugar
1 package vanilla sugar
1 pinch of salt
1 egg
200 g margarine
2 egg white
100 g powdered sugar
100 g hazelnuts
100 g walnuts
100 g chocolate decoration (droplets)
Powdered sugar, for dusting

preparation
Make a shortcrust pastry from flour, 100 g ground hazelnuts, sugar, vanilla sugar, salt, 1 egg and margarine, then chill for 30 minutes.

Beat 2 egg whites until stiff, add powdered sugar. Fold in 125 g ground hazelnuts.

Mix the hazelnut kernels, walnut kernels and chocolate drops.

Roll out dough, cut out circles with a glass (diameter approx. 7

cm). Add 1 tsp. of egg white mixture to each circle, then cover with the nut-chocolate mixture. Fold up the cookies (leave half open, do not close).

Bake for about 15 minutes at 200°C

After cooling down, dust with powdered sugar.

BAKED APPLE CASSEROLE WITH MARZIPAN

vegetarian

Working time approx. 15 Minutes
Cooking/baking time approx. 40 Minutes
Total time approx. 55 Minutes

557 calories

ingredients
For the casting:
100 g marzipan paste
2 egg
50 g sugar
300 g crème fraîche
1 package of vanilla sauce powder

Also:
4 medium sized apples
Raisins
Grease for the mould

preparation
Dice marzipan for the glaze. Mix with eggs and sugar with a blender until creamy. Stir in crème fraîche and sauce powder.

Wash, halve and core the apples. Fill raisins into the bowls. Place apples in a greased baking dish with the raisins facing upwards. Pour the glaze over it.

Bake in the preheated oven (top/bottom heat: 200 °C, fan oven 175 °C) for approx. 35 - 40 minutes.

Serve with vanilla ice cream or cream or both.

RUM BALLS

vegetarian

Working time approx. 30 Minutes
Rest period approx. 6 hours
Total time approx. 6 hours 30 Minutes

2745 calories

ingredients
100 g butter
300 g dark chocolate
2 tablespoons cocoa powder
4 tablespoons rum
Chocolate shavings or chocolate sprinkles

preparation
Mix softened butter, grated chocolate, cocoa and rum to a smooth mixture. Form balls of about 2 cm diameter and turn them into chocolate sprinkles. Then refrigerate for several hours.

MOUSSE AU CHOCOLAT WITH ORANGE SCENT

vegetarian

Working time approx. 30 Minutes
Rest period approx. 16 hours
Total time approx. 16 hours 30 Minutes

ingredients
4 eggs (very fresh)
1 package vanilla sugar
250 g chocolate, semi-bitter
250 ml whipped cream
40 ml orange liqueur, (Cointreau)
1 Orange, (only the abrasion of the peel)
1 pinch of salt
Mint, for decoration

preparation
Separate the eggs. Beat the egg white with a pinch of salt until very stiff. Beat the cream until very stiff. Beat the egg yolk with the vanilla sugar until very frothy. Stir in orange grated butter and orange liqueur.
Melt the chocolate in a water bath and add it to the egg mixture while stirring. Carefully stir in first the very stiff beaten egg whites, then the very stiff whipped cream in portions. Leave to set overnight in the refrigerator.

To serve, cut off the cams and garnish with mint leaves.

COCONUT COOKIES

vegetarian

Working time approx. 15 Minutes
Cooking/baking time approx. 10 Minutes
Total time approx. 25 Minutes

1072 calories

ingredients
200 g margarine
200 g sugar
200 g flour
200 g grated coconut
1 egg
½ Package baking powder
Grease for the sheet metal

preparation
Mix all ingredients with the mixer. Use a teaspoon to cut off small piles and place them on a greased baking tray. Press the heaps flat.

Bake in a preheated oven at 200 °C top/bottom heat for 10 minutes.

Please make sure that the piles are really small, because the mass will run apart when heated and the cookies will become too big!

WELFENSPEISE

vegetarian

Working time approx. 10 Minutes
Rest period approx. 3 hours
Cooking/baking time approx. 20 Minutes
Total time approx. 3 hours 30 Minutes

ingredients
For the cream:
500 ml milk
40 g sugar
1 package vanilla sugar
40 g starch flour
4 egg whites, beaten stiff

For the foam
4 egg yolks
80 g sugar
250 ml white wine
½ Lemon, juice thereof
1 tablespoon starch flour

preparation
Bring milk and sugar to the boil (keep 5 tablespoons of it). Stir the starch flour into the 5 tablespoons of remaining milk, add it, bring to the boil briefly. Fold egg whites into the hot cream and fill into a glass bowl or glasses.

For the wine mousse, put all ingredients in a pot (do not use aluminium!). Heat over half the flame or circuit 2 while beating vigorously. Allow everything to boil briefly, then take it down and continue beating briefly until it has cooled down a bit. Pour the wine mousse onto the cooled cream and refrigerate until ready to eat.

SOUR CREAM - KRINGEL WITH SUGAR

vegetarian

Working time approx. 30 Minutes
Total time approx. 30 Minutes

ingredients
250 g flour
4 tablespoons sour cream, sour cream or sour cream
250 g butter, cold
75 g sugar

preparation
Put the flour, sour cream and butter in pieces in a mixing bowl. Knead the ingredients first with the hand mixer, then with cool hands briefly and vigorously. Chill the dough in cling film for 30 minutes.

Roll out the dough on a well floured work surface to a thickness of approx. ½ cm. Cut out circles (approx. 4 cm diameter) with a round cookie cutter. Cut out another circle (approx. 1 cm diameter) from the middle of each circle to form curls. Knead the dough again, cut out a total of approx. 60 circles.
Press the circles slightly into the sugar, spread the smooth side of the circles on 2 baking trays lined with baking paper. Bake the trays in the preheated oven (electric oven: 175 °C/circulating air: 150 °C) for 15 - 18 minutes.
Enough for about 60 pieces

PUMPKIN SEED CROISSANT

vegetarian

Total time approx. 35 Minutes

ingredients
300 g flour, smooth
200 g butter, room temperature
100 g powdered sugar
100 g pumpkin seeds, finely ground
1 package vanilla sugar
1 pinch of salt
1/2 teaspoon cinnamon
some lemon peel, untreated, rubbed
Flour for the work surface
possibly grease for the sheet metal
as desired couverture, dark chocolate, melted

preparation
Knead all ingredients except the chocolate coating with a mixer (or with your hands) to a smooth dough and leave to cool for half an hour.

Then form small croissants on a floured work surface and place them on a greased or baking tray covered with baking paper. Bake in the preheated oven at 180°C top/bottom heat for about 12 minutes. Let cool down.

After cooling down, dip the tips of the croissants into the melted dark chocolate coating. Place on a baking tray and let the chocolate coating cool down.

Tip: If the dough does not join together immediately (this may be due to the flour), simply knead in a tablespoon of cold milk, this always works!

SPICE BALLS

vegetarian

Working time approx. 45 Minutes
Rest period approx. 1 hour
Total time approx. 1 hour 45 Minutes

ingredients
200 g butter, soft
3 egg yolks
100 g powdered sugar
1 package vanilla sugar
1 pinch of salt
1 teaspoon gingerbread spice
200 g flour
1 teaspoon baking powder
30 g cocoa powder
125 g hazelnuts, ground
100 g cake glaze, whole milk
Pistachios, chopped (as desired)
Flour, for moulding

preparation
Butter Place the egg yolks, powdered sugar, vanilla sugar, salt and gingerbread spice in a bowl. Mix everything with the whisks of the hand mixer until foamy.
Sift in flour, baking powder and cocoa powder and sprinkle the hazelnuts over it. Mix all ingredients with the hand mixer to a smooth dough. Cover the dough and refrigerate for one hour.
Line the baking tray with baking paper.
Turn the dough into walnut-sized balls with floured hands and

place them on the baking tray at a distance of 2-3 cm. Chill for 10 minutes.

In the meantime, preheat the oven to 175 °C.

Bake the cookies in the oven for 10-15 minutes. Put them on a cake rack to cool down.

Chop the icing into small pieces and melt in a potty in a hot water bath. Dip the domes of the cookies into the icing and sprinkle with pistachios as desired. Let the glaze dry for 20 minutes.

SHORTBREAD COOKIES

vegetarian

Working time approx. 15 Minutes
Rest period approx. 12 hours
Cooking/baking time approx. 20 Minutes
Total time approx. 12 hours 35 Minutes

ingredients
1 kg Mehl
500 g Zucker
500 g Butter
8 Packung Vanillezucker
2 Esslöffel Öl
1 Teelöffel Backpulver
4 Ei
1 Packung Kuvertüre oder Schokolade zur Deko

preparation
Knead all ingredients to a smooth dough. Cover the dough with a kitchen towel, leave it to rest overnight, not too hot and not too cold.

The next day, put it through the mincer with the pastry attachment. Place on baking trays lined with baking paper and bake at 200 °C convection oven or 220 °C O/U for about 20 minutes.

Variation: After cooling, dip the cookies in chocolate couverture, allow to dry and then fill into tightly sealed tins.

CHRISTMAS-COOKIES

vegetarian

Working time approx. 30 Minutes
Cooking/baking time approx. 12 Minutes
Total time approx. 42 Minutes

4047 calories

ingredients
150 g butter
180 g flour
90 g sugar, white
90 g cane sugar, brown
100 g hazelnuts, chopped
1 egg
150 g chocolate, (chocolate droplets)
½ teaspoon baking powder
1 teaspoon cinnamon powder
1 pinch of salt
1 package vanilla sugar

preparation
Preheat the oven to 175°C.
Beat the soft butter with the egg, sugar, cinnamon and vanilla sugar until fluffy. Mix the flour with the baking powder and the salt and add it. Carefully stir in the chopped hazelnuts and chocolate drops. Place small heaps of the dough on a baking tray with a teaspoon. They will later run into round cookies, so make sure there is enough space.

Bake on the middle shelf for about 12 - 14 minutes. Let the

cookies cool down and store them in a tin.

LEBKUCHEN PARFAIT WITH RED WINE PEAR

vegetarian

Working time approx. 1 Stunde
Rest period approx. 4 hours
Total time approx. 5 hours

ingredients
For the parfait:
1 teaspoon gingerbread spice
100 g gingerbread with chocolate without wafers
2 egg yolks
125 ml milk
1 vanilla pod
75 g sugar
4 cl rum, brown
250 g whipped cream
Fruits: (red wine pears)
8 Pear
100 g sugar
¼ Liters of wine, red
125 ml port wine, red
125 ml orange juice
3 lemon, the juice
6 cl liqueur (cassis liqueur)
some cinnamon, whole
1 bay leaf, brown
2 carnation

preparation

Gingerbread parfait:

Cut gingerbread into small cubes. Boil up the milk with the vanilla pod, let it stand for about 15 minutes, let it cool down a bit. Cream sugar and egg yolks, sift the vanilla milk with the gingerbread spice into the egg yolk mixture and mix.

Beat everything over steam until warm, until about 65° C. Beat cold in an ice bath until a thick, viscous cream is formed. Fold in the rum, the diced gingerbread cubes, then fold in the stiffly whipped cream. Pour into moulds and freeze for at least 4 hours.

Red wine pear:

Pears (small Abate, Williams, Santa Monica, etc.) Cut out or halve and drill out the core.

Caramelize sugar. Deglaze caramel with red and port wine and dissolve. Add orange and lemon juice, spices, prepare some lemon peel like mulled wine.

Pour in the peeled and prepared pears, add the cassis, cook slowly, turning so that the pears become evenly red. Lightly thicken the stock with a little bit of starch and sieve it.

To serve, pour a saucepan on a large plate, place the parfait on top, cut half a pear smooth at the bottom so that it can be placed upright next to the parfait. Sift the powdered sugar over the plate, possibly sprinkle some chocolate chips over it.

NUSS-NOUGAT-STANGEN

vegetarian

Working time approx. 1 hour
Cooking/baking time approx. 10 Minutes
Total time approx. 1 hour 10 Minutes

5499 calories

ingredients
For the dough:
225 g butter
100 g powdered sugar
1 package vanilla sugar
3 egg yolks
1 teaspoon cinnamon powder
200 g wheat flour
40 g baking cocoa
1 teaspoon baking powder
125 g hazelnuts, ground

For the filling:
100 g nut nougat cream
For the casting:
150 g dark chocolate
30 g coconut oil

preparation
For the dough:
Cream the butter and gradually add the sieved powdered sugar,

vanilla sugar, egg yolks and cinnamon.

Stir in the flour mixed with cocoa and baking powder and sieved by the spoonful. Finally fold the hazelnuts into the dough. The finished dough is best brought into the typical pastry form with the help of a mincer with a pastry attachment. The dough sticks should be about 4 cm long.

Place the resulting dough sticks on a baking tray covered with baking paper and bake in a preheated oven at 175 °C for 7 - 10 minutes. If the dough sticks are a bit too wide, you can cut them in half lengthwise with a small knife while still warm.

For the filling:
Stir the nut nougat cream in a small pot over low heat on the stove until smooth. Spread half of the cooled cookies with the nougat mixture on the underside using a baking brush, place the rest on top and press down well.

For the icing:
Crush the chocolate and stir it together with the coconut oil over a bain-marie to a smooth mixture. Brush the ends of the sticks with it.

WHITE RUM BALLS

vegetarian

Working time approx. 30 Minutes
Rest period approx. 1 hour
Total time approx. 1 hour 30 Minutes

ingredients
80 g butter
2 tablespoons of cream
200 g chocolate, white
10 ladyfingers
8 tablespoons rum, brown
6 tablespoons almond, chopped
100 g almond, in flakes

preparation
Melt butter in cream at low heat. Remove pot from the stove. Let the liquid cool down slightly. Dissolve the chocolate in the lukewarm liquid while stirring.
Caution: The chocolate curdles easily if the butter-cream mixture is too hot. Let it cool down. Put the cookies in a plastic bag and roll over them with the rolling pin until they are crumbled. Soak the crumbs with rum. Roast chopped almonds without fat at medium heat in a pan. Mix with the cooled chocolate mass and the sponge-rum crumbs. Cool for about 60 minutes. Form small balls from the solidified mass. Roast the flaked almonds without fat. Roll the rum balls in it. Put them into praline moulds. Store in a cool place.
Enough for about 40 pieces.

YEAST MEN

vegetarian

Working time approx. 30 Minutes
Rest period approx. 1 hour
Total time approx. 1 hour 30 Minutes

451 calories

ingredients
500 g flour
1 cube yeast, fresh
60 g sugar
200 ml milk, lukewarm
60 g butter, soft or margarine
1 pinch of salt
1 egg, size M
1 squirt of lemon juice
For brushing:
condensed milk
Egg Yolk

preparation
Place all ingredients in a bowl and knead. Then leave to rise for 1 hour in a warm place.

Knead dough well, roll out and cut out alarm clocks. Leave to rise for another 15 minutes on the baking tray and then brush with condensed milk and egg yolk.

Put the clay pipes in your arm.

Bake in a preheated oven at 200 degrees for about 17 minutes.

ANISE BUTTONS WITH CHOCOLATE

vegetarian

Working time approx. 30 Minutes
Rest period approx. 1 hour
Total time approx. 1 hour 30 Minutes

ingredients
210 g flour
160 g butter
2 egg yolks
60 g sugar
1 package vanilla sugar
100 g chocolate flakes
1 teaspoon aniseed, ground
Cake glaze (whole milk or lemon)

preparation
Cream softened butter, continue stirring with sugar and egg yolk. Then add the remaining ingredients, form small balls and place them on a prepared baking tray. Press flat with a fork and bake at 160°C convection oven for about 15-17 minutes.

Cold with milk glaze, in which you can stir in aniseed powder to taste, or glaze half with lemon glaze.

CHOCOLATES - CRÈME BRÛLÉE WITH SPICY ORANGES

vegetarian

Working time approx. 45 Minutes
Rest period approx. 2 hours
Total time approx. 2 hours 45 Minutes

ingredients
150 g chocolate coating, plain
250 ml milk
250 ml cream
100 g sugar
½ tablespoon rum
6 egg yolks
3 Orange, untreated
75 ml grenadine
50 g sugar
300 ml orange juice
1 stick of cinnamon
2 star anise
3 Cardamom capsule
1 clove
1 vanilla pod, (the pulp of which)
1 teaspoon of cornstarch
4 tablespoons sugar, brown

preparation

Break the couverture into pieces.

Bring milk, cream and 100g sugar to the boil and remove from the heat. Add couverture pieces with the rum to the milk-cream mixture and let it melt while stirring.

Preheat the oven to 110 degrees.

Stir the egg yolks one after the other into the chocolate-milk-cream mixture and stir over a hot water bath until creamy. Then pass through a fine sieve.

Pour the chocolate cream into flat moulds and cook in the oven for about 1 1/2 hours. Keep cool for about 2 hours.

Cut wafer-thin strips from the skin of an orange. Let them simmer with grenadine for about 15 minutes. Peel all three oranges carefully with a knife and fillet them.

Caramelize 50 g sugar light brown (attention: hot!) and fill up with orange juice. Add cinnamon, star anise, cardamom and vanilla pulp and reduce by half.

Mix the starch with a little cold water and thicken the orange-spice stock with it. Put the pot aside and let it cool down a bit. Then add orange fillets and zests and chill.

Sprinkle the chocolate crème brûlée with brown sugar, caramelize with a Bunsen burner and serve with the spiced oranges.

RED WINE COOKIES

vegetarian

Total time approx. 1 Stunde

72 calories

ingredients
500 g flour
250 g sugar
280 g butter
1 tablespoon cinnamon
2 tablespoons cocoa powder
6 tablespoons wine, red
1 egg
1 package baking powder

preparation
Knead all ingredients together and then chill the dough. Cut out round cookies and bake at 175 degrees for about 12 minutes. Make a glaze with powdered sugar and red wine and spread it on the cookies. Makes about 70 pieces.

BALSAMIC - NUT - PIECES

vegetarian

Working time approx. 35 Minutes
Rest period approx. 8 hours 30 Minutes
Cooking/baking time approx. 15 Minutes
Total time approx. 9 hours 20 Minutes

ingredients
120 g nuts, ground
4 tablespoons balsamic vinegar
300 g flour
130 g sugar
1 package vanilla sugar
1 pinch of salt
200 g butter, soft
1 egg
vanilla sugar to taste, to roll

preparation
Heat the balsamic vinegar in a pot and add the nuts, mix well and leave to stand overnight.

The next day, knead all ingredients into a smooth dough. Cut the dough in half and shape each into a roll. Sprinkle some vanilla sugar on the work surface and roll the rolls in it until they are well covered with the sugar all around.
Wrap the rolls in cling film and put them in the freezer for about 30 minutes.

Cut the rolls into slices about 4 mm thick and place them on the tray.

Bake at 160 degrees (fan oven) for approx. 12 - 15 minutes until lightly browned.

CHRISTMAS CHOCOLATE

vegetarian

Total time approx. 20 Minutes

ingredients
200 g chocolate coating, semi-bitter
200 g chocolate coating, whole milk
200 g nougat
100 g butter
1 teaspoon butter-vanilla flavor, liquid
¼ teaspoon cardamom, ground
¼ teaspoon cloves, ground
2 teaspoons cinnamon
100 g walnuts, roughly chopped

preparation
Coarsely chop the couverture and melt it with the nougat and butter in a hot water bath - stirring, as it will otherwise set slightly. Mix in spices and walnuts. It is best to fill into a square stainless steel mould and let it cool down. Always keep in the refrigerator.

MULLED WINE CAKE WITH CINNAMON CREAM TOPPING

vegetarian

Working time approx. 45 Minutes
Rest period approx. 1 Stunde
Total time approx. 1 hour 45 Minutes

ingredients
For the short pastry:
220 g flour
1 teaspoon baking powder
100 g butter, cold or margarine
80 g sugar, also brown if desired
1 egg, (size M)
1 bag of vanilla sugar
1 teaspoon cinnamon powder

For the filling:
2 glasses of sour cherries, large
850 ml mulled wine
125 g sugar
2 bags of pudding powder, chocolate
150 g chocolate decor, (chocolate chips)
For the hood:
500 ml cream
2 bags of vanilla sugar

4 bags of cream stiffener
2 tablespoons cinnamon-sugar mix or
2 tablespoons chocolate sprinkles

preparation
Prepare a shortcrust pastry from the dough ingredients and line the bottom of a springform pan (26-28 cm) with it, pull up the rim properly, prick several times with a fork, chill for about 1 hour.

For the filling, drain the cherries (or put them into the mulled wine the night before), take off some spoons of the mulled wine and mix the pudding powder with it. Heat the rest of the mulled wine with the sugar while stirring. Add the pudding powder to the hot liquid and bring to boil. Let it boil for 1-2 minutes while stirring constantly. Remove the pot from the heat and fold in the well drained, tipsy cherries. Finally, carefully and quickly fold in the chocolate chips. Pour the hot mixture onto the cold short pastry.

Bake the cake in the preheated oven at 180° (hot air) for about 35-40 minutes. Let it cool down overnight, or better 24-48 hours, so that the mixture gets firmer. Can be prepared very well before the holidays.

Before serving, with the stiffly whipped cream, place generous thick patches next to each other. Finally, powder with cinnamon sugar.

COCOA COOKIES WITH CHRISTMAS SPICES

vegetarian

Working time approx. 45 Minutes
Rest period approx. 30 Minutes
Cooking/baking time approx. 12 Minutes
Total time approx. 1 hour 27 Minutes

4319 calories

ingredients
125 g butter
200 g sugar
2 egg
50 g cocoa powder
1 teaspoon cinnamon powder
½ teaspoon clove powder
½ teaspoon nutmeg
300 g flour
½ Package baking powder
Flour, for the work surface

For the casting:
250 g powdered sugar
4 lemon juice, possibly less

preparation

Mix all the ingredients together and make a kneading dough. The dough should be smooth and not sticky. Put the dough in the fridge for about 30 minutes.

Roll out the dough on a floured work surface about 0.5 cm thick and cut out any figures. Place on a baking tray covered with baking paper.

Bake at about 175°C for about 12 minutes.

Mix powdered sugar with lemon juice until a thick icing is formed. Always start with a little lemon juice so that it does not become too liquid.
Make sure to cover the cookies with icing so that they become soft. Allow the icing to dry well and then keep the cookies in well sealed tins.

CHRISTMAS DESSERT

vegetarian

Total time approx. 15 Minutes

460 calories

ingredients
200 g gingerbread
100 ml cherry juice
1 glass of cherry
200 g quark
200 ml cream
100 g powdered sugar
50 g chocolate sprinkles or chocolate shavings

preparation
Drain the cherries and collect the juice. Crumble the ginger-bread, add the cherry juice and mix. Mix the quark and pow-dered sugar, whip the cream and fold into the quark mixture.

Now fill quark mixture, then gingerbread mixture, cherries and again quark mixture into glasses. Finally, decorate the dessert with one cherry and the chocolate shavings or chocolate sprin-kles.

Keep cool until serving.

CORNFLAKES – BISCUITS

vegetarian

Total time approx. 30 Minutes

4880 calories

ingredients
200 g butter, soft
180 g sugar
2 eggs (size M)
1 package vanilla sugar
350 g flour
½ Package baking powder
5 cup cornflakes
100 g chocolate, grated

preparation
Beat butter with sugar, vanilla sugar and eggs in a large mixing bowl until foamy.
Sift the flour and mix it with the baking powder and gradually stir it into the foamy mass.
Work the cornflakes and the chocolate under the dough, preferably with a large wooden spoon, otherwise the mixer would reduce the cornflakes too much.

Preheat the oven to 175°C.

Form small cookies from the dough on a baking tray lined with baking paper, then bake for about 15 minutes.

VANILLA PEAR WITH CHOCOLATE-MARONIC CREAM

vegetarian

Total time approx. 40 Minutes

343 calories

ingredients
8 Pear
1 liter pear juice
1 vanilla pod
1 stick of cinnamon
2 tablespoons honey
1 lemon
100 g chocolate
1 egg
200 g chestnut . puree
2 sheets gelatine
250 ml cream

preparation
Peel and halve the pears.
Boil up pear juice, scraped vanilla, the cinnamon stick, honey and squeezed lemon juice, poach the pears in the stock until soft.
Melt the chocolate, mix with the egg and add the chestnut puree.

Soak the gelatine in cold water for about 2 minutes, then squeeze it gently, fold it into the chocolate mixture, then fold in the whipped cream, chill for about 30 minutes.
Put the maronic cream into a piping bag and squirt it into the pear halves, garnish a little!

QUARK BALLS

vegetarian

Working time approx. 45 Minutes
Cooking/baking time approx. 30 Minutes
Total time approx. 1 hour 15 Minutes

ingredients
400 g flour
500 g low-fat curd cheese
250 g sugar
4 egg
1 teaspoon of salt
1 package baking powder
1 tablespoon vanilla sugar
1 vanilla pod, pulp scraped out
1 lemon (organic), grated zest

Also:
3 cups of clarified butter for frying
150 g sugar
2 teaspoons cinnamon

preparation
Cream the eggs with the sugar for about 3 minutes. Add quark and salt and stir for another 1 minute. Add all the remaining ingredients and stir until the flour has been worked in properly.

Heat the fat in a pot. When you can see bubbles on the wooden spoon, you can put the first mice in: Using two teaspoons, slide the dough into the hot fat in portions. Important: do not let the fat get too hot!

Fry the mice for 2 - 3 minutes until they have a golden brown color.

After baking, let the balls drip off on kitchen paper and then roll them in plenty of cinnamon sugar or just dust them with powdered sugar.

The recipe makes about 80 quark balls.

ALMOND CAKE

vegetarian

Total time approx. 20 Minutes

6143 calories

ingredients
1 cup of cream
150 g sugar
2 cups of flour
3 egg
1 package baking powder
1 pinch of salt
some vanilla sugar
200 g butter or margarine
150 g sugar
300 g almond
4 tablespoons of milk

preparation
For the dough, mix together the cup of cream, 150 g sugar, 2 cups of flour, 3 eggs, 1 packet of baking powder, pinch of salt and some vanilla sugar. Then bake the dough on a baking tray covered with baking paper for 10 minutes in a preheated oven at 200°C.

In the meantime make the almond paste with 200 g butter or margarine, 150 g sugar, 300 g almonds and 4 tablespoons milk. Bring the almond paste to the boil and pour it on the dough. Then bake the cake again for 10 - 15 minutes.

BAKED APPLES IN WALNUT COAT

vegetarian

Total time approx. 20 Minutes

311 calories

ingredients
5 apples, each approx. 150 g
75 g butter
75 g sugar
50 g nuts, ground
½ teaspoon cinnamon
Cinnamon, whole

preparation
Peel the apples and cut out the core from the middle with a core cutter.
Melt the butter and turn the apples several times.
Mix sugar with nuts and cinnamon and turn the apples in the mixture until they are completely covered with it. Put them into a casserole dish.
Add the rest of the nut mixture to the remaining butter and mix.
Spread the mixture into the holes in the middle of the apples.
Insert 1/2 to one whole cinnamon stick each and cook at 180°C for about 45-50 minutes until a nice golden yellow crust is formed.

The baked apples taste best hot with vanilla, walnut or caramel ice cream.

The sauce created in the casserole dish can be served over the ice cream.

CINNAMON ICE CREAM WITH PEARS AND GINGERBREAD SAUCE

vegetarian

Total time approx. 25 Minutes

416 calories

ingredients
3 egg yolks
75 g powdered sugar
1 teaspoon cinnamon
2 tablespoons rum
250 ml cream
For the sauce: (gingerbread sauce)
70 g chocolate (dark chocolate)
250 ml cream
1 teaspoon gingerbread spice

For the fruit:
2 pears (4 halves), steamed
some lemon juice
some sugar

preparation
Beat the egg yolk with powdered sugar until foamy. Whip 250

ml cream until stiff and fold into the egg yolk mixture together with cinnamon and rum. Fill into a mould and put in a freezer for at least 2 1/2 hours.

Peel and halve the pears and remove the core. Steam in water with some lemon juice and sugar to taste, then drain and let cool.

For the sauce, heat 250 ml cream with the dark chocolate and stir in the gingerbread spice.

Arrange the cinnamon ice cream with the pear halves on plates and serve with the gingerbread sauce.

Made in the USA
Las Vegas, NV
09 December 2023

82408684R00115